WALKING ON THORNS

WALKING ON THORNS

*Discovering the
Meaning of Suffering*

BY JEANNE G. MILLER

Copyrighted Material

Walking on Thorns: Discovering the Meaning of Suffering

Copyright © 2015 by Jeanne G. Miller.
All Rights Reserved.

No part of this publication may be reproduced, stored in a retrieval system or transmitted, in any form or by any means—electronic, mechanical, photocopying, recording or otherwise—without prior written permission from the publisher, except for the inclusion of brief quotations in a review.

For information about this title or to order any of her other books, contact the publisher:
Jeanne G. Miller
PO Box 6907
Tyler, TX 75711
life_interrupted@hotmail.com

ISBN: 978-0-9910805-2-6 (print)
       978-0-9910805-3-3 (eBook)

Printed in the United States of America

Cover design: Miladinka Milic • www.milagraphicartist.com
Interior design: 1106 Design

This book is dedicated to my parents, for without their support and dedication to my progress, I would not have reached my potential.

To my biological mother for her gift of life.

And to both sets of parents for showing me
what true sacrificial love looks like.

Table of Contents

Introduction . . . . *ix*

Chapter 1
Starting at the Beginning *1*

Chapter 2
What's Wrong with Me? Will New Skills Help? *5*

Chapter 3
Fire! *13*

Chapter 4
A Lack of Trust *25*

Chapter 5
Not Another Defect! *31*

Chapter 6
High School *51*

Chapter 7
Two Blind Dates *63*

Chapter 8
The Light of Life *71*

CHAPTER 9
Why Has God Forsaken Me? 91

CHAPTER 10
An Awakening 113

CHAPTER 11
A New Kind of Education 129

CHAPTER 12
Everything is Connected 153

CHAPTER 13
Healing of Memories 175

CHAPTER 14
Death and Resurrection 181

CHAPTER 15
Example of Brokenness 193

CHAPTER 16
Healing with Dreams and Other Blessings 203

CHAPTER 17
A Grateful Spirit 227

CHAPTER 18
Putting It All Together 235

CHAPTER 19
Stories from the Other Chair 245

CHAPTER 20
It Is Your Turn 255

Reflections from Jeanne's Journey 263

Introduction

Acceptance of one's life has nothing to do with resignation;
it does not mean running away from the struggle.
On the contrary, it means accepting it as it comes,
with all the handicaps of heredity, of suffering,
of psychological complexes and injustices.

—PAUL TOURNIER

It was a few years ago now. I went with a purpose, a mission it had taken me a lifetime to fulfill. I placed the flowers at the head of her grave, nature's gift of living beauty that was a testament to hers.

I silently greeted her and then just stood there in timeless contemplation. And then I started to talk to the mother I had never met in life but had come to know in death.

I thanked her for conceiving me and for taking the pregnancy to full term.

I thanked her for giving me up for adoption to two people I loved and trusted with all my heart.

I thanked her for my life.

I honored her for the burdens she had carried on my behalf.

I regretted that she would never be able to tell me personally about her relationship with my birth father but I shared with her what I had learned about him on my own.

I told her how I thought I was like him.

I told her how I thought I was like her.

I told her that I was no longer angry with her.

I told her that there was part of her that I carry inside of me every day.

I told her I loved her.

On leaving her grave that day, I felt a sense of celebration and the completion of a circle of events that shaped my destiny. I felt as though I had discarded the heavy burden of confused identity. As I got back into my car, a calm peace descended on me and tears of real joy began to flow. I realized that I had taken another step on my journey of transformation and fulfillment.

The person that I have come to be has been transformed through the pain of many wounds and personal suffering. I have endured shame, guilt, disgrace and humiliation. I have been detested, arrested, molested and, most of all, tested. I am a psychotherapist, a mother, a wife, a spiritual director and an ex-alcoholic. I have experienced excruciating, unbearable physical trauma and even worse emotional pain. In the end, however, all of those horrors and disappointments, failures and miseries, have evolved into blessings, gifts of healing and the recognition of what life truly offers

As I have walked through the struggles, the relationships, the experiences, the choices and the inherent challenges, I have learned that nothing has been wasted. I am certain of the truth that every event requires choices and all choices have led and will continue to lead me to become the person I was intended to be.

In a maze, there are dead ends that require one to turn around and possibly backtrack. There are many possible paths once in the maze. Wrong turns and blind alleys are common. So is getting lost or disoriented. Whereas mazes are mental linear, left-brained experiences, a labyrinth's path is soothing, rhythmic and meditative. Think of a maze as rationality and a labyrinth as intuition.

A labyrinth is different in that all experiences are part of the entirety of the whole journey. To walk the labyrinth's path, it is necessary for me to follow a path through an intricate pattern until I reach the center. Once reaching the center, I go back out in the same manner. The center of the labyrinth is where I discover the answers to the questions that I am asking. In psychotherapy terms, it is the discovery of the self.

Life for me is the labyrinth. This book is not just about *my* journey inward and back out again, but everyone's. And I hope my experiences and observations will resonate with you, have meaning for you and speak to you. I don't have all the answers but I have a lot of the questions; these are included at the end of the book by chapter to help you examine your own journey.

I believe every event that we experience, every choice that we make and every emotion that we feel are all part of the ever-developing master plan. Looking back into my past gave me an opportunity to honestly face my life and to make changes where required. When I was stubborn or too fearful to look at a given situation, I found I increased my misery and multiplied the misery of others. Sometimes life presented events I did not choose but how I responded to those events was my choice. When I allowed the healing process to evolve, transformation could occur in ways that were mysterious and beyond joyful. The joy came only after the hardship of facing the pain.

As a psychotherapist, as a spiritual director, and as a pastoral care assistant, I have heard story after story that testify to the fact that adversity is often a lonely experience. In the pages of this book, you will read other stories that have been shared with me as recognition of the fact that transformation is a common challenge, characterized by unique experiences and variable results.

> *When I allowed the healing process to evolve, transformation could occur in ways that were mysterious and beyond joyful.*

Everyone has a story to tell about his or her life. While the events of those lives may be similar to one another, the combination of events and characters makes each story unique. The way something happened, how it was perceived and other variables make every life different. Different events have helped to form the course of each life path. While these details may differ, the shared possibility of the transformative power of each person's struggles make each life a story worth telling.

In my own journey and from the stories that I have been told, there were events or insights that brought us to our knees in both surrender and supplication. I call such a humbling event a *spiritual challenge*. This challenge offers the opportunity to do the most difficult thing that can be asked of us: step outside the bounds of the primal brain and the ego and cross over to another side where there is a different view of events and of self, one based on openness rather than reflexive, primitive defense. These events trigger the search for answers to questions such as: Why am I here? Who am I? Why did this happen to me? Is there something greater than myself? What do I believe about life and my faith? Is there a God, and if so who or what is it? If there is no God of creation, then what do I put my faith in: money, self, government or possibly science?

The questions themselves produce a kind of a crisis. Some people are born asking them. However and whenever you arrive at the point in life when your search begins, there is the opportunity to discover wholeness and a higher calling for your existence. It calls for literally transcending the brain's dictates and evolving into a spiritual self.

Coming face to face with oneself can be earth-shattering. Sometimes, it's easier to avoid the mirrors. Searching one's soul to find true identity and to accept the answers to the questions takes courage. When understanding is found, it takes courage to stay in the search that might take a lifetime. The search doesn't just take place in the mind but also in the body, the emotions and in the faith. It never ceases.

At times, it may seem like giving up is the only way to stop the pain. Our default setting is to be guided by the primal brain with its focus on survival and safety. The brain has distinct areas, all having evolved at different times. At the lowest levels are the control of fundamental functions like breathing and primitive responses to threat designed to ensure survival. At the more evolved levels are the abilities for more sophisticated thinking and behavioral control. But the primitive brain dominates, especially during the tough times which pose a threat to our survival. The challenge is to somehow override those primal responses even when every cell in our body is demanding we defend ourselves, especially when we are vulnerable.

Feeling exposed can often cause a profound need to cover up again. The excuses to stop are endless. Change in and of itself causes a crisis and the brain wants to avoid a crisis at all costs. Those significant people in your life are also influenced by your change. Because of their own uncomfortable feelings about the changes they see in you, they may attempt to create an environment so that you can return to the old familiarity with them. Are the pain and the confusion that are experienced in discovery and growth worth it? *Yes.*

"Why?" you might ask.

Moving beyond the ego and its master, the selfish, primitive brain, allows us to develop real self-awareness and accept the truth.

This has the potential to set us free so we can live unchained to our past. Then we are free to embrace the person that we were designed to be. Denial can be replaced by acceptance, resentment with forgiveness, and dread with hope. For me, the influences of early childhood overflowed into adulthood. I emotionally ran from that little girl and symbolically hid her in the closet. I neglected her by trying to run away from all the hurts. I ran because I had no human contact to help me along the way. God the Father became the friend who sustained that lonely little girl and raised her into womanhood where she could rediscover the child's pain. I was so focused on surviving all the different challenges that I lost sight of my talents and innate potential. They remained concealed from me until the challenges were resolved, at which time I awoke to discover the Jeanne that had always been there. The healing of my childhood and the effects those wounds had in adulthood allowed me to be at one with myself, a different self. I felt that I had transcended the primal brain and evolved into something more sacred, though I have to admit there's a thin line between scared and sacred, especially when you're dyslexic.

The warring inside has ended. The running has ceased. The hiding has turned into openness. These changes allow me to risk using the talents that I was born with and to celebrate the life that I was given.

So I share my life story with you, the reader, as a guidepost to your own search for meaning and transformation. It is designed as an encouragement when you need to move through any painful situation, which requires that you come out of the dark closets of your life to find your radiant healing. I share my story because life, no matter how hard it may seem, is a gift to be discovered.

Chapter 1

Starting at the Beginning

Childhood is a tricky business. Usually, something goes wrong.
—MAURICE SENDAK

I was born in a small town in Texas, in 1947, to a birth mother who was emotionally and financially unable to care for me. She placed me in foster care until she could restructure her life to make a home appropriate for me to live. I had an older sister and the burden of another mouth to feed was frightening. However, my birth mother came to the realization that her community would never accept her for having a child from a man other than her husband, nor me for being illegitimate. I was seven months old when she decided to relinquish her parental rights. Esther, a social worker from the Fort Worth area, knew about Mother and Dad's intent to adopt children. Therefore, she called them to offer my placement with them.

Dad said later that when he and mother came into the room, he saw me sitting in Esther's lap. I looked up at him, smiling from ear to ear, let out a squeal of delight and reached out to him with both my arms opened wide. He said that he melted in love, picked me up into his arms and emotionally bonded with me forever more.

A college graduate, Mother believed in scholastic excellence as a goal to be accomplished. She was beautiful, gracious and full of compassion. She chose a life of service to her community and to others. She gave her money away in the form of gifts to persons, organizations and worthy causes. She put persons, whom she felt would appreciate the education, through school when their personal funds were lacking. She gave of her own money to begin an Episcopal elementary school. She was an accomplished violist and sat as second chair in the local symphony. She always enjoyed having her friends drop in for a visit. Her friends and anyone who met Mother found it easy to admire and to love her. She was an example of graciousness.

Part of her graciousness manifested itself in the belief that she had to keep the peace at whatever cost was necessary. Victorian in nature, she held in her emotions, never talking about them. She had a healthy self-esteem, which may have hindered her ability to relate to me. Her extremely positive outlook, however, brought about in me the feelings of not being able to measure up to her.

Dad was funny, a University of Texas graduate and witty. He loved to play tennis, to fish and to read. In his early business career, he was part of his family's business and then, after WWII, a pilot for an airline. After the family sold the business and he was no longer employed as a pilot, he purchased a private airplane and farmland. He loved to fly his plane. He would take us places and it was always an adventure to remember. He was wise and had an uncanny ability to read a person's intent. He loved his close friends and loved to tease them. He was an active member of the local Rotary Club. He loved nature and open spaces. He was a successful provider for the family; however, he lacked the healthy self-esteem needed to accept his successes. He had mood swings that led to depression and irrational behaviors. Eventually, he became trapped in the cycle of alcoholism. While there he could be scary and threatening. I was confused, because when he was drinking, the father who loved me disappeared.

> *The path to a more evolved life requires an understanding of the forces that shaped you.*

The path to a more evolved life requires an understanding of the forces that shaped you. It's impossible as a young child to see one's parents as anything but parents. With age, I was able to shed the childhood lens and to see them more clearly as people with their own lives, as individuals not parents. Then I could understand them more fully and revisit my perceptions of them. This task is especially meaningful for adopted children, almost all of whom have some fantasy as to who their birth parents were and why they were given up for adoption. Sometimes they can find those parents and seek those answers directly; sometimes indirect means are necessary; and for some there's never the opportunity to discover the facts, leaving the question unanswered.

Parents are obviously a huge influence on every aspect of a child's development. The family network also exerts a huge influence. The roles I played in my family as I was growing up had an impact on the relationships that I have had throughout my life. Understanding who my parents were, their personalities, motivations and predispositions, helped clarify their influence on me and I could only do that through the lens of an independent adult not a dependent child.

Chapter 2

WHAT IS WRONG WITH ME? WILL NEW SKILLS HELP?

*Children with disabilities are stronger than we know,
they fight the battles that most will never know.*

—MISTI RENEA NEELY

Birthdays are generally fun but my fifth birthday was really memorable. On the day itself, my mother wasn't at home. She was in the hospital. So on the morning of my birthday, the maid got my sister Martha and me ready and drove us ten minutes to the hospital where Mother was confined. When we got to the hospital we were told that we were too young to go to the second floor. We had to wait.

We were impatient. Waiting wasn't something I wanted to do on my birthday. Eventually, my mother's nurse appeared. We could see her through the glass doors of the elevator. Mother wasn't there. But Chad, my baby brother who was born just a few hours before, was! He looked so small. Martha and I jumped up and down, waving and generally introducing ourselves to the sleeping bundle of love, now wrapped in the anonymous nurse's lucky arms. Dad just stood and watched, silent, joyful tears appearing on his cheek, temporarily rendering words obsolete.

Now that I was five, it was time for me to start kindergarten. I enjoyed being with the other children, especially playing on the swings, slide and jungle gym. We would run around in a state of blissful freedom. Another favorite part of the day came after nap time. That's when the milk and cookies appeared. Then it was back down to kindergarten business, which included learning to identify letters, pronouncing their sounds and making words. I didn't know it at the time but these were the first steps on a very painful journey.

I continued to enjoy kindergarten but toward the end of the year the teacher expressed concern to Mother about my progress. She was particularly concerned that I was having some difficulty processing letters. I tended to switch them and write them sdrawkcab—backwards. She told Mother to follow my progress closely.

First grade was an upgrade. The building seemed huge, with many stories and fun places and rooms to explore. There were many children, too, each with their own stories and I had a lot of fun making friends with them. There were also a lot of books with stories and that was turning into a big problem.

In kindergarten, the teacher used phonics to teach us to read. But now, the first grade teacher taught us using flash cards with whole words to memorize. To remember the word, I had to see all the letters in their proper order and decipher what they meant. Without the sound cue for the letters, my brain needed extra time to visually process them, convert them into sounds and create the word. However, because my visual processing of letters was compromised, this technique didn't work very well. Moreover, I was not given the extra time I needed, yet I was expected to keep up with my classmates. I soon began to fall further behind.

At this time in education, there was very little recognition of special needs. If you had difficulty with a specific mental function, like visual processing, you were just seen as "slow" or, even worse, stupid. There was little or no attempt to understand the impact of a specific deficit on overall performance. The teacher failed to recognize that my inability to recognize words was a function of a very specific deficit. As a result, there was no attempt to help beyond the exhortation for me to try harder. But the harder I tried, the worse I became, or more specifically, the worse my reading became.

But I was getting worse. The more I tried, the more mistakes I made. More attempts were simply an invitation to fail more. The mere repetition of something you can't do makes you realize how much you can't do it. Frustration and anxiety set in, neither of which helped my performance. Of course, they made *it* worse. They made *me* worse.

Looking back now, I could see that at this age my performance defined how I thought about myself. My self-definition came from what I could and couldn't do. Eventually, I was able to make the perceptual transition from seeing myself as a set of skills to viewing myself as a whole person with value beyond a set of abilities. But that would come later. My dyslexia didn't have anything to do with me as a person. I consciously didn't cause my difficulties. They were just there. My brain didn't work the way most others did when it came to visual processing. Naturally, I interpreted that to mean there was something wrong with me. If I had a broken foot and couldn't participate in gym class, no one would have mocked me, least of all myself. But you can't see the brain and you assume that it is you. The more I believed that I was defined by my performance, the more pressure I felt to succeed. My failure was a reflection of me.

Holding my train of thought was difficult. Many times, even as I was talking, my mind would go blank and my thoughts would simply disappear. Because I felt so embarrassed, it was difficult to reclaim my thoughts or my words. The anxiety was crippling. It was like some toxic fog that threatened to poison every attempt to communicate. I was mortified and I felt so *different* from everyone else. I was beginning to feel like an outsider.

My handwriting was a mess, a reflection of my processing difficulties. I added extra letters that did not belong. I left out necessary ones. I reversed letters and numbers. At times, my brain would consolidate letters to make a word that had no meaning. I needed extra time to process the thoughts into usable information. Another idiosyncrasy was that my brain would sometimes picture an answer before the words could form, a sign of intuitive processing. However, if I tried to consciously convert that answer into words, my speech became scrambled.

I made so many mistakes that my failure dominated my mind, prompting many questions. Why was I so different? What was wrong with me that I could not perform like the other students? Why did the teacher pick on me? This pressure, of course, made my performance worse. I experienced firsthand the crippling effect of anxiety on trying to do almost any action. It was like having the cruelest critic on my shoulder watching every movement. I would have to learn how to silence that critic if I was to ever have a chance of improving my reading skills.

> *I made so many mistakes that my failure dominated my mind, prompting many questions.*

I believed that other students, and certainly the teacher, thought I was inadequate. But perhaps more importantly, *I* felt I was inadequate. I also felt guilty because I sensed that my teacher was holding me responsible for not succeeding. It was all my fault but no one was telling me how to fix it.

As the year progressed, the students began to make fun of my mistakes, heaping more shame and guilt on my first-grade shoulders. All this ratcheted up my anxiety even more, if that was possible. I was afraid I would make a mistake even before it happened, which made it more likely that I would.

The teacher's response to the fact that my visual processing problem had prompted an emotional collapse was to punish me for both. Instead of seeing a specific learning difficulty, she saw lack of effort. Instead of remediation, there was impatience and blame. She sat me on a high stool in the corner of the room for not paying attention and not trying. What was truly sad was that I was trying my very best and it was plain to everyone, but especially to me, that my best was not good enough. I was confused and lonely. The high stool, where I was placed, was above all of the other students' desks, and everyone saw me sitting there, conspicuous by my inadequacy and stupidity. I felt *shame* for the first time in my life.

The shame came from the fact that I believed others were seeing and judging me as inadequate. This was no longer a private criticism, it was a public humiliation. The criticism that others gave me was not as bad as the criticism that I gave myself but it certainly reinforced it. Now there was simply no escape from it. The idea was firmly planted in my brain that everyone was looking down on me all the time. Whenever I was in class, I felt as if I had a huge mark on my head that said 'idiot.' I was in a bubble of disgrace and inadequacy and I could see no way out.

My mother conferred with my former kindergarten teacher about the difficulties that I was experiencing in the first grade. The teacher suggested that Mother find a copy of the McGuffey reader series for her to use as homework in an effort to increase my familiarity with words and reading. The McGuffey readers were written to inspire high scholastic standards in the areas of grammar, vocabulary and reading.

Mother began reading bedtime stories to Martha and me. Being together was comforting and my mother would sometimes play bedtime stories that were written to music on the piano. We had a lot of fun singing along. But the fun stopped when she asked me to read aloud from the McGuffey reader. I made so many mistakes, mispronouncing the words and forgetting their meaning. I was once again mortified, ashamed and embarrassed. Mother tried her best to help me but I felt like a hopeless case. My stupidity was no longer confined to the classroom. My shame was complete.

It was all beyond my comprehension.

There was no way that I, or any child of five, could have worked out how to understand the problem and fix it. That is not possible. All the efforts that were made, from my well-meaning mother to the mean teacher, just made me worse. Perhaps I could have had more support, or be shown a way to fix the problem, but that would not have stopped me feeling the way I did.

It would take me a long time before I could generally accept that I am not my brain. Through no fault of my own, my brain worked differently. Then it responded to the internal and external criticism in a way that only compounded the problem. How could I ever find a way to circumvent these natural tendencies, and find a way to rise above it?

Chapter 3

FIRE!

Shame is the most powerful master emotion.
It's the fear we're not good enough.

—BRENÉ BROWN

When I was seven years old, I would sneak into my parents' room after they went to sleep. I needed to be close to them to feel security, comfort and acceptance. I would sleep on the couch in their bedroom, snuggled under the couch cushions. The cushions hid my presence in case they woke in the middle of the night. I would sneak back into my bedroom just as the sun was coming up. I needed as much comfort as I could get before I got to school.

My third-grade teacher was a work of cruelty. I was inquisitive, quick to learn new information by experience but I was exceptionally slow to read or to learn from books. I continued to write backwards, leaving out words or letters and condensing sentences into strange combinations of letters that, in my mind's eye, was a complete sentence. My brain worked faster than my hand could write. I had the same problem with talking. I became the class scapegoat, a child, it seemed, who did not pay attention and did not want to try to learn. In response, shame continued to overshadow my actions.

I developed self-doubt about what I could do. I was afraid to make a direct statement, as it might be wrong. To me, silence was less threatening than speaking. The teacher saw me as defying her and decided quickly that she was not going to like me. She publicly humiliated me before the class for making mistakes until I was in tears. Even after the tears, I would have to stay after school and write, "I will pay attention to the teacher while in class" what seemed like hundreds of times on the blackboard.

The next morning, as the students entered the classroom, they could see the blackboard full of *"I wlil pay ateteniotn toe trechre whin calsl. I wlil pay ateteniotn toe taechre whin calss."* There are no words to describe the humiliation I felt. I would become nauseated, my heart would race and my face would flush. I had to hold back tears, which made my throat hurt from the strain. It was a combination of shame, panic and helplessness with a lot of sadness and loneliness thrown in for good measure. Because I was afraid of making a mistake, I would spend a lot of time trying to anticipate a mistake and how to cover it up. The pressure was enormous and I had to find some way of coping with the emotional turmoil. Most of my coping was intuitive and a natural response to very unnatural circumstances.

I began to daydream and withdraw emotionally to protect myself from the threat of being humiliated. I spent much of my time alone, climbing trees or taking solitary walks through the neighborhood. I would hide in the chest where all of our toys were kept in the corner of my closet or behind the clothes, hoping no one would see me cry. I dissociated and it often felt as if I were watching myself going through the motions from outside of me.

That same year Mother found a reading tutor for me. I had to leave school at the appointed time and walk a few blocks to the tutor's home. My third-grade teacher would cause me to be late. If I got up at the correct time and left class, I got in trouble and again would be publicly humiliated before my fellow students, repeating the usual routine of staying after school to write hundreds of times on the blackboard whatever she wanted me to say. The words were always there in the morning for all the students to see.

I don't think anyone knew how desolate I felt. My strategy had become the avoidance of the immense emotional pain by whatever means necessary. I continued to find ways to hide my emotions from others and, hopefully, from myself. Crying to myself was a way for me to release my shame, but even crying was shameful for me. I believed crying only showed even more weakness. Therefore, I sought out a place of isolation to cry. This solitary place protected me emotionally from my fear of being disapproved of by others. I was learning the art of emotional concealment. I was learning to completely hide all of my feelings and became adept at showing a stoic presence in order to hide my sadness, anxiety and desperation.

I could play with my classmates, cousins or family like other children my age. However, I held in all the pain and agony of my shame, self-doubt and loneliness in some other part of myself.

In fifth grade, (1957–58), after I had a long series of neurological and psychological tests, I was diagnosed with a learning disability called dyslexia. Finally, there was a name, albeit a Greek one, for kids like me who couldn't read English. A condition with a name, even a foreign one, sounds legitimate. And if it was a legitimate condition, maybe there was a legitimate cure. I was taken out of public school and sent to the only school in town that had special reading programs, which could help me learn to read. It was sensitively named "the school for the physically and mentally retarded" (it really was called that back in the late 1950s). That term "retarded" has had a long-lasting effect on my psyche.

On my first day going to the new school, I was up early. I was ready and eager to learn to read. Then I would be like everyone else. I would blend in with my classmates and my family and I'd be accepted! I would get approval from everyone! No one would make fun of me anymore. Goodbye ridicule. Goodbye self-doubt. Goodbye isolation.

As I walked up the sidewalk to the entrance of the school, however, I found myself among students who labored with spastic paralysis as they walked and others who had a difficult time forming words to communicate. I was mortified that I was now identified as belonging to this group who were even more on the fringe than I was. My soul screamed from within that I was not like these students. Oh…but wait! Perhaps I was like them and I had always been wrong about that, too. Emotionally traumatized by the sight of the other students and my association with them, I was unable to learn anything. My hope and my dream of being normal were shattered before my eyes. I slipped into believing at a very deep level that I was truly mentally retarded. I must be or why else would I be there at that school? The misplaced hope of normalcy did more damage than I could imagine. I would have been better off staying where I was and being publicly humiliated in a regular school. There, the humiliation seemed limited to my teacher and my classmates. Now the whole school system and society at large seemed to agree that I was a hopeless misfit, a pathetic "retard."

The belief that I was damaged grew stronger. The notion had been an outpost in my head but it had just received major reinforcements. The experiences in my new "school," simply confirmed beyond a shadow of doubt, that I would never be any different. I had been created this way and there was no way to change the way I was formed. I felt I had no one to talk to about my feelings. No one took the initiative to talk to me about how my value as a person was separate from my special needs. My hope of reading and being able to fit in with the rest of my classmates was shattered. This little lonely child cried in agony inside.

To survive emotionally in public, I had to develop a strategy of denial, minimizing, covering up, blocking out or disconnecting from the truth of my feelings. Hiding behind these defenses had allowed me to pretend that everything was all right. I could no longer pretend. My sense of shame overpowered me and I felt lost. The trauma of being in that school was more than I could handle.

I became so downcast that I began to have suicidal thoughts. Disapproval and chastisement were far greater emotional burdens than death would ever be. I never told anyone about my thought to end my life and I was too lonely and embarrassed to ask for help. Ironically, it was a deep sense of failure that saved me that day from making a serious decision to end my life. I was only ten and already carried a deep sense of shame and isolation from the world that overshadowed all of my feelings and thoughts. To cope, I cried alone. Words cannot describe the loneliness that I felt, for it went into my bones, into my heart and into my soul. What ten-year-old contemplates suicide? This was a very perilous time in my life.

Mother was aware that my mood had become withdrawn and I began to carry my body in a bent-over manner from the weight of my burdens. We never discussed my feelings. I don't know whether that was a function of my unwillingness to discuss feelings or hers. I didn't know how she would have reacted to finding out her daughter was suicidal and I'm not sure how she perceived my emotional state. Obviously, I didn't trust telling her. However, she must have had some sense of my unhappiness as she saved me by putting me back in public school. It must have been hard for my mother to return me to the public school knowing that there would be no further help in teaching me how to read.

The following summer (1958), I had the opportunity to go to camp. I looked forward to it, as the summer could be so boring.

Camp Waldemar offered many activities to do. I could "do" things successfully and camp was the place to "do" things. Because I grew homesick, I would write home often. When I did, however, Mother would send the letters back to me with the misspelled words *corrected*. I just knew that all the other campers could see these letters and the corrections. I felt like there was nothing that I could do to win her approval and I feared the teasing from the other campers.

No one at camp knew that I could not read or spell. I wanted a place where I could escape the others knowing about these deep, dark secrets I hid. I was so humiliated. Martha was at camp with me. She did not get any letters sent back. I felt, and could justify by now from experience, that I was not loved as much as my sister. The camp term was six weeks long. I soon stopped writing letters to avoid repeated humiliation. If I were a lot older and smarter maybe I might have realized that I had just learned one of the fundamental principles of communication: if you want people to communicate with you, you must make them feel safe and secure enough to do so.

Words cannot describe the loneliness that I felt, for it went into my bones, into my heart and into my soul.

Fortunately, dyslexia had not affected my coordination. I was limber and could do almost anything physically. I loved climbing trees, riding horses, ballet, jazz dancing, water-skiing, roller-skating and tumbling on the trampoline. I had the courage to be in the recitals for ballet. I quit taking piano lessons as I was unable to get through the stage fright of knowing that I had to perform in front of others. I knew that the entire audience would hear my every mistake. There was no way for me to hide from the sound of wrong notes as they filled the room. Discord would be everywhere.

I loved the outdoors. I loved to go to my ballet lessons. I could get lost in the twirling and the sensation of floating. I would go fishing with my dad, play out on the farm or walk in the woods. Competitive sports were out as I was emotionally unable to compete. Self-consciousness undermines any sporting endeavor and doubt kills any possibility of success. My creative talents were expressed in my participation in the Garden Club for juniors where I won awards for my flower arrangements.

> *I had a special talent for putting things together. I was gifted with strong eye-hand coordination.*

Our family continued to attend the Episcopal Church, where I was taught all the Bible stories during Sunday school. I trusted with a child-like faith the truths found in those stories. I could identify with Moses and Joseph, as they were born of one family and raised in another. Moses also had a speech impediment and often pleaded with God that he was the wrong man for making historic announcements. But God reassured him that he would be able to deliver. I accepted that God had a plan for my life, too, and that His intervention was part of that plan. I sang in the choir and, when I was big enough, I became an acolyte.

I also had a special talent for putting things together. I was gifted with strong eye-hand coordination. The Christmas of my sixth-grade year (1958–59), my parents gave Chad a cardboard jail playhouse. Martha, now twelve, said that she could put it together. She was advanced beyond her age group in her ability to read, spell and write. She got out all the pieces and laid them very carefully on the floor; she then got out the instructions and proceeded to read them. I looked at the pieces, looked at the finished picture and took action to put it together long before my sister had finished reading the instructions. I could win approval for doing things or remembering details or directions from experience, but not from academics. There, Martha excelled. She was a straight "A" student and never had to study very hard. I wasted so much time comparing myself to her. I was envious of her success and the ease with which she seemed to achieve it.

Every year our Christmas tree stood with stately magnificence in the front entry hall where our spiraling staircase ascended gracefully to the opening at the second story balcony. When I was twelve, we had an especially tall and beautiful tree. We put all our lights and trimmings on it. We actually had to go to the attic and get down the extra lights that we had not needed in previous years. As a family tradition, we did not take the tree down until New Year's Day. This particular New Year's Day (1960), the family had been at the tennis courts where everyone, except for me, played tennis.

I liked to watch; it was my escape from competition. You can't make a mistake watching.

Once home, we all went upstairs to get out of our tennis clothes. I was dressed first, so I started back down the stairs. As I did, I noticed a flicker in one of the light strands on the Christmas tree. It reminded me of the flame that appears when someone flicks his or her cigarette lighter. The flame suddenly grew brighter.

I screamed for Dad, "The Christmas tree is on *fire*!"

Dad stepped into the hallway from his bedroom and saw the small flame. He grabbed a blanket off his bed and threw it on the tree. Mother stopped changing out of her tennis clothes to call the fire department. There was too much air under the blanket for it to smother the flame. Dad asked me to go quickly downstairs and unplug the lights from under the tree before the flame got any bigger. I ran down the stairs, but by the time I got to the bottom, the tree was in full blaze.

I screamed, "I can't get under the tree to unplug the lights. I'm scared!"

This was a crisis moment. I just ran out of the house. I sat on the curb, rocking back and forth and crying. I was terrified! I was afraid that Mother, Dad, and Chad would burn to death, as they could not get out. I believed that because I was too scared to get under the tree to unplug the lights, I had caused the fire to get bigger. I froze in fear out on that curb.

Then I saw the housekeeper come up the driveway in her car. I shouted to her that the house was on fire. She jumped out of her car, leaving it to run into the flowerbeds before it stopped. She then ran inside toward the fire. I instantly blamed myself for sending her into the fire and possibly causing her harm. I blamed myself for being out of control and screaming in fear. My sense of inadequacy and self-hatred was more out of control than the fire.

Our house had two staircases. The grand circular one stood in the front hall and a second smaller and narrower one was hidden at the back of the home. To save their lungs and lives, the family crawled on the floor and down the back stairs to safety. Dad was able to get a garden hose and, with the housekeeper's help, extinguish the fire before the firefighters came. Even though the smoke damage was extensive, only the Christmas tree had caught fire.

After he had put out the fire, Dad came and rescued me off the curb. He kept reassuring me that it was okay that I did not get under the tree to unplug the lights. Dad could be so understanding. I wasn't. I just kept *blaming* myself.

Chapter 4

A Lack of Trust

Learning to trust is one of life's most difficult tasks.
—ISAAC WATTS

One weekend when I was in the fourth grade, Mother went out of town. She normally left Martha, Chad and me in the care of our housekeeper, but this weekend it was Dad's turn to care for us. Dad's routine pattern of alcohol consumption had increased over the past several years and had begun to scare us, but this particular weekend was dramatically different. He came home from the farm already agitated and disoriented. He began to rage against Chad, who was just acting like a normal four-year-old. Dad started screaming obscenities at us about whose children we were and continued yelling, "I wish that you had never been born. I will kill you." My brother started crying and ran to his room. Dad went to get his gun and then ran after him continuing to scream, "I will kill you."

Martha and I ran to save our brother. We gathered him up, ran to the bathroom and locked the door. Dad found us and pounded on the door as he continued to shout. He kept yelling those obscenities, this time threatening to knock the door down as he shouted, "I will kill you all." The longer he yelled, the more enraged he became. We were all huddled in the bathroom, trembling with fear. We had never seen Dad this scary before and we did not know what was going to happen. What if Dad did break the door down? What would happen to us? What if he shot through the door and hurt one of us? We had to get out of the house.

We tied sheets together and let ourselves down from the second story window. We ran for our *lives* to the neighbor's home. Chad did not stop crying until we were safe. When we returned home the next morning, Dad did not remember how he had acted the night before. When Mother returned from her trip we told her, but she indicated she thought we were making it up.

I was confused. What was happening to our family? Dad was becoming more violent toward us and especially toward his son. This is the same son, only a few years earlier, Dad had been so proud of when he was born. Mother pretended that a problem did not exist. The truth we had experienced was in sharp contrast to the words of a trusted parent, who said nothing believable happened.

Dad's drinking continued to increase. He took most of his rage out on Chad. I remember hearing Dad curse at Chad and say all kinds of degrading things. I remember when Dad attempted to kill Chad by holding him under the water while fishing. There happened to be some other fishermen who came by, saw what was happening and stopped Dad from drowning Chad. I have memories of Dad holding a loaded gun, pointing it at Chad and screaming that he wished that Chad had never been born. Mother would jump in between them to keep Dad from shooting. I remember Dad screaming at the top of his lungs in the grocery store at Martha that he wished that she had never been adopted. I felt so guilty that I could not stop his behavior. I was afraid that something would happen to Mother, Martha or Chad. I loved and hated my dad at the same time. His behavior scared me intensely when he was drinking. When he was sober, he was funny and I thought he had a great deal of wisdom. Whenever I would go to him to talk to him, when he was sober, he would listen and give me counsel that I could understand.

There was always a part of me that held back, just in case.

Dad loved to fish. He would take me from time to time. We always had fun. He would bait my hook and take off the line all the fish that I caught. I felt special on these trips. My fishing trip experiences were so different from the ones that Chad had. I yearned for more times when Dad was calm. But my trust had been eroded. I could never be completely sure of how he would react. There was always a part of me that held back, just in case. His unpredictability had violated the three keys of a loving relationship; respect, safety and honesty.

The summer after the fourth grade (1956–57), we were on our usual family vacation in the Colorado mountains. We rented a duplex so that Mother, Dad and Chad were on one side and Martha and I were on the other side with Myrtle, the housekeeper, who always went with us. As a treat, Mother would give Martha and me fifty cents to go to the five-and-dime store to buy something. Martha would ask that I share one-half of my money with her so she could save hers. I wanted my sister's approval so badly that I would let her have whatever I had or do almost anything she wanted so I could win her favor. She would return with all of her money still in her pocket. I would get into trouble each time for allowing this transaction. I was the person in the wrong for having a gullible heart. I do not remember Martha ever being reprimanded for being the manipulator.

That same summer, another incident influenced my understanding of my value and how my needs could be met. I liked to sleep on the screened-in porch of our rented cabin. It would get cold at night, so I would nestle down under the covers. Most times, I would pull the warm covers over my head and snuggle down toward the foot of the bed.

One night, I was awakened abruptly as Martha pulled me out of my warm sleeping position to reposition me at the head of the bed where it was cold. I told her to go away and leave me alone. She went back to her bed. I snuggled back down at the foot of the bed under the warm covers and went back to sleep. Then again, I was awakened as the result of her pulling me back out of the covers.

I shouted, "Leave me alone!" I was so angry with her for bothering with me. She proceeded to say that she needed me to be at the head of the bed. That was where I was supposed to sleep. Then she went back to her bed. By this time, I was so very angry that it took me awhile to calm down enough to rest. I hated being awakened in the middle of the night and especially being bothered. I hated being told what I ought to do by Martha when it was not my choice. It seemed like hours, but I was finally able to get back to sleep at the foot of my bed under the covers. To end it all, I was awakened a third time by her demanding that I sleep at the top of the bed and not under the covers at the foot of my bed.

I yelled, *"Leave me alone!"* and ran to wake Mother. My running into her room with Martha running behind me startled Mother. Martha sat quietly with a grin on her face while I frantically explained why I was there. I was talking so fast that I had to repeat myself a couple of times. In desperation, I asked Mother to tell Martha to stop waking me and to leave me alone. Mother just looked at me. I said it again: that I needed her to tell Martha not to wake me. Mother spoke directly to me and told me to go back to bed and Martha would not bother me anymore. I did not trust that Martha would stop bothering me of her own choice. I was even more desperate, and I began to cry, pleading that she would specifically direct Martha to *"stop."* Mother said nothing.

I shouted: "I will scream until you tell Martha to quit bothering me!"

Mother just looked at me and then rolled over and pretended to be going back to sleep. How could she turn away from my need to have Martha leave me alone? I was powerless to do anything about keeping Martha away from me while I was sleeping. I did not even think of defending myself by hitting her; I would have been blamed for it. I needed Mother to protect me. I screamed the rest of the night, standing at the foot of my mother's bed. She played opossum but did nothing. Mother, too, had violated the fundamental principles of trust: she didn't honor my feelings by ignoring them and she opted for the easy way out rather than dealing with the issues honestly. Who was I ever going to trust?

Chapter 5

Not Another Defect!

*The acknowledgement of our weakness
is the first step in repairing the loss.*

—THOMAS à KEMPIS

Halfway through my eighth-grade school year (1960–61), I began to complain of pain that went from the lower back through to the hip area and on down to the ankle. I had developed a physical problem of unknown origin, which influenced my ability to learn and added to my already struggling self-esteem. Because of all the different expressions of dance in which I was involved, my ballet teacher thought that I had pulled a muscle. I stopped tumbling on the trampoline, dancing jazz, which I dearly loved, and acrobatics, but not ballet. The pain continued. I stopped horseback riding and water skiing. I stopped climbing trees and hiking. The pain continued to intensify over time. My disappointment continued to increase as I was forced to let go of the things that I loved, the very activities that were my coping strategies, the activities that gave me my self-esteem. I was not gifted academically, but in the physical, I had a sense of accomplishment that had somewhat offset the failures in reading and school performance. Finally, I had to even stop my beloved ballet. I was becoming a blob of pain without anything that I could call "me."

The pain shifted from just being uncomfortable to keeping me awake at night. I would rock my entire body back and forth in the bed each night in order to fall asleep. This rocking helped to reduce the burning pain and the muscle cramps. Soon I was not able to walk without a limp due to the increased level of pain. I hurt sitting, walking, sleeping and generally all the time. The pain cramped, burned, throbbed, darted, tingled and ached deeper than I could identify.

I had mentioned this pain to my mother a number of times. After a month, she became concerned, so she took me to the pediatrician.

He agreed that I must have pulled a muscle, and rest from all activity was prescribed. However, the pain and the limp did not go away. I lost the natural rhythm of walking. My grades began to suffer, as I could not focus on anything except how badly I hurt or how sad I was in facing all the losses. I was overly self-conscious about the ever-intensifying limp and the differences in how each leg moved. I was confused and unable to identify where the confusion was coming from. In May, when it was time for me to have a physical and immunizations before going to camp, I returned to the doctor. He was now concerned about doing something serious about my pain; he referred me to a local orthopedic surgeon. After an exam and several x-rays, he diagnosed me as having a "slipped capital femoral epiphysis" (damage to the bones in the hip socket). The surgeon referred me to a famous clinic in New Orleans for a consultation. The doctor in New Orleans agreed with the orthopedic surgeon in my hometown. Surgery was scheduled to secure and stabilize the hip joint.

The dynamic with my mother meant that sometimes I probably didn't convey how much pain I was in and she never asked me. Her plate was already full. Her friends and social obligations were important to her. She was dedicated to her commitment to her duplicate bridge group and she cherished her giving of her talent as a violinist in the Symphony. What little energy she had left was spent sweeping Dad's drinking under the carpet. It was something we never talked about. Dad continued to attempt to kill my brother through the years but I did not know about these events until I was an adult. My sister required an exorbitant amount of attention from mother; she was anxious and fearful. Between the needs of my sister and my brother, there was not much time for me. I felt very much alone and isolated from the nurturing care of those around me. It was the maid, who was also the cook and our nanny, who was the one who was my friend. I trusted her.

Mother cried when she heard the diagnosis. That was only the second time that I had ever seen my mother cry. Years later, she told me she was so sorry. She felt responsible for the severity of deterioration and for the problems I was to face in the future. Maybe she was responsible because she let it go on so long or maybe she saw the path I was headed down and realized it would be difficult. I was only thirteen and had no idea what path I would be walking, perhaps limping, down. Mother knew. She had to build a tough stance toward my physical recovery. At the time, I thought she did not care about or love me. I was basing that on an already established belief that I was not worthy of her love. Had she been overly protective of or overly sympathetic to me, I would never have learned to walk or learned how to live with pain. God's grace gave my mother the ability to be strong in the face of both of us hurting. Since it was her nature to hide like an ostrich and avoid dealing with truth, she may have been strong because she was faced with no other choice. She had worked diligently to become an accomplished violinist and knew the rewards of hard work. It took her a lifetime of practice. Mother could not see the emotional pain I experienced from a reading disability. She saw the mistakes. However, she could see the pain in my physical handicaps and ultimately responded to me with compassion and strength. Once she told me a story about a friend of hers whose son had had polio. The doctors

> *I was only thirteen and had no idea what path I would be walking, perhaps limping, down.*

had told her friend to place their son in the middle of the back yard and allow him to crawl to them. They were instructed not to go get him even if he began to cry for them. Mother's friend said she sat on the patio in tears watching her son struggle to reach them. Day after day this continued until he was strong enough to walk. Mother said that if her friend had not been so strong she would have keep her son handicapped for his entire life. This was a message I could relate to. I wish we had more conversations like this. I was given hope and purpose for all the struggles where I felt so alone.

A slipped femoral epiphysis is an unusual, although not rare, disorder of the adolescent hip. For reasons that are not well understood, the ball at the upper end of the femur (thigh bone) softens and slips off in a backward direction. A slip occurs because the growth plate between the epiphysis and the rest of the thigh bone cannot stand up to the stress placed upon it. Most often, it develops during periods of accelerated growth, shortly after the onset of puberty. Usually, the slipping of the epiphysis is a slow and gradual process. However, it may occur suddenly and be associated with a minor fall or trauma.

It occurs two to three times more often in males than in females. Early diagnosis provides the best chance to achieve the stabilization of the hip and reduction of future complications. The most common complications include the permanent alteration of blood supply to the femoral head (called avascular necrosis) and a loss of articular cartilage of the hip joint (referred to as chrondrolysis). Loss of articular cartilage may cause the hip to stiffen with permanent loss of motion, loss of ability of the joint to bend, shortening or shrinkage of a muscle or tendon and chronic pain.

Depending on the severity of deterioration of the epiphysis, surgery may be required in order that the surgeon can place pins in the hip to stabilize the socket. Depending on the severity of the destruction of the non-weight-bearing joint, at least three or four months may be required to ensure that the abnormal growth plate has fused. Placing pins through the socket to stabilize the joint has a side effect. The pins actually stop any further growth of the femur. The epiphysis of the femur is one of the growth joints for body height of the bones. With physical therapy, some range of motion can be regained. If the deterioration is minor, normal activities can be resumed. On a continuum, the more severe the destruction of the socket, the less range of motion can be regained and the less activity will be recommended. I had been diagnosed in the severe stage of deterioration.

I left the doctor's office on crutches so as not to put any weight on the leg until the bone had hardened. With today's modern medical advances, I might not have been required to be non-weight-bearing for as long as I was, or maybe at all. The crutches felt awkward. I was unsure of my balance. I could ride a bike very well but balancing on crutches was another matter. Once, I lost my balance and fell. The fussing from my parents began with passion. From then on, they fussed about me. Even though I did everything for myself, they hovered around me, smothering me with anxiety. Because of the significant degree of deterioration, I was advised to have surgery.

A few weeks into the summer of 1960, the surgeon placed three long metal pins in my hip socket. The surgeon told me that because the pins were placed in the hip socket, there would be no more growth in my leg from hip to knee but that there would be from knee to ankle. It would be necessary for me to remain non-weight-bearing until the bones had hardened again. Even though I was educated about this, I was unaware of how my body would look with one leg shorter than the other and how that would affect my self-esteem. I did not understand the visual reality of one leg shorter than the other. I had no idea what "shorter" would be. I was thirteen and did not have any experience in knowing how to process the reality. I knew that it was awkward to maneuver around on the crutches and it took some time to get used to using them with comfort. Fortunately, the school year had just ended and that gave me the summer to adjust to my new situation.

I was unaware of how my body would look with one leg shorter than the other and how that would affect my self-esteem.

My self-esteem continued to suffer. I found it difficult to accept all the losses I was having to face and experience. I had lost the ability to do all the physical activities that I enjoyed. I lost my identity of being physically whole. I lost the affirmation associated with ballet. I lost my ability to focus on play or activities. I was consumed with pain both emotionally and physically. I began to feel useless. Doing things had been my only way of developing some sense of self-esteem. I could not succeed in school. Now I was having my ability to get around to do things taken away from me. I was scared and felt uncertain about the future. I think I was locked into loss and didn't realize it. Maybe there was some shock that blinded me for a time as I struggled to cope with the unknown.

To help me find something to do from a sitting position, Mother found a woman who could teach me to sew. In learning to sew, I discovered something new to do for which I had a natural talent. I naturally saw where the pieces were to go. I did not need the pattern except for cutting the fabric. I soon moved away from bought patterns and began to design my own.

Dad suggested I take apart one of his suits to learn how to make finer garments. I began making everything from my own clothes to party dresses, and later, my husband's suits, my children's clothes, curtains and country quilts. I enjoyed the creativity of it, but I was not emotionally capable of believing how good I really was. My ears were deaf to believing someone would be telling the truth if I was given a compliment. I didn't trust it. The junior high school I attended in the seventh and eighth grades was in a two-story building with no elevators. It was necessary for me to transfer to the other junior high because it was handicapped-accessible to complete the ninth grade. By the time school started, I was tired of crutches. I had fallen down enough times to know that I was ready to ditch them. My hands had blisters on them and my underarms were sore. I dropped things often. I never got used to the noise when something hit the floor. I was mortified when I was in public and I dropped something. I did not like the feeling that I was handicapped.

Once school started, other students noticed my situation and asked questions that made my self-consciousness increase. Some students were concerned about how they could help while others made fun of me. Because I was already supersensitive about criticism, I magnified the negative comments. When I became too tired for the crutches, I would switch to a wheelchair. It was easier to balance my schoolbooks and purse from a sitting position. I was self-conscious in that wheelchair but there was also part of me that was grateful that I was not confined to living in the chair.

Mother had the shoe repair person design a leg brace that went across my left shoulder and down to the right foot, holding it up and off the ground. When using crutches, this brace kept me from spontaneously putting weight on my leg. It was embarrassing to wear this brace. It went right between my breasts and distorted my blouse. Shoulder purses were not in style in my town; I was out of the mainstream in fashion. I was thankful I did not have to wear the brace when I was seated in the wheelchair.

All junior-high-school-age children worry about what others think. I wanted and hated the attention I received. I wanted it because it helped me to feel valuable; I hated it because I feared others were either just pitying me or mocking me. I held my feelings about my situation quietly in my heart. I was embarrassed about being dyslexic and now about my physical disability. "Smile, and pretend that everything is under control." That was my family's motto. And it became mine as well.

I kept others away emotionally as I pretended that everything was fine. If I talked about my true feelings, I would cry, and that would just add to the shame and embarrassment. Whenever I moved close to facing all my losses, I felt myself and all my defenses begin to crumble. I feared being defenseless and I would shut the door to those emotions. I shut the door to allowing them to surface. I was so worried about what others saw. All the issues surrounding dyslexia, and now this silly brace, crutches and the wheelchair, just intensified how inadequate I felt. All the losses became one big disappointment to carry. I would get angry and sometimes sit at the top the stairs in our home and let my crutches plop one step at a time all the way down to the bottom. It sounded like I was falling down the stairs. Mother would come running and be really angry with me for scaring her. I was just plain mad that I had to be the way I was. We never talked about my "mad" and how it was related to loss or any other emotion. This was my way of crying out for help and no help came.

After seven months on crutches, the doctor said I was ready for the pins to be surgically removed (December 1961). I was on crutches one more month after recovering from the actual surgery. Then the surgeon said I could walk again (January 1962).

Great news! Walk again! No problem, right? I was not prepared for the pain to increase. I had been in pain for the last year. Even when I was non-weight bearing, my hip hurt. Like an arthritic joint, weather affected it. No medicine had been prescribed. I would complain quietly and, as a result, no one else had any idea as to the degree of pain that I was feeling. Physical therapy had not been prescribed to help develop my muscles to support my leg. Eight months on crutches had left my leg exceptionally weak.

I began to walk with a terrible limp. My entire body dropped to one side as I put weight on the right leg. I pictured myself as walking like the Hunchback of Notre Dame, which isn't a positive image for a teenager. The muscles fatigued and cramped quickly. Pain continued, not only because of the bone but also because of the muscles. I did not know anything about pain management. No one ever addressed the issue of pain management with me. All I could do is deny, cry or fidget. It was too painful to sit still.

The right leg was shorter than the left. The shape of the leg was noticeably different in form and size. The right leg had atrophied from disuse. The reality that the femur was not growing was now evident. I saw what the surgeon had told me would happen. I felt so deformed, twisted, misshapen and visibly imperfect. Out of a deeply buried fear of being abandoned, I grew up needing to have the approval of my family. Striving for perfection was my subconscious

Out of a deeply buried fear of being abandoned, I grew up needing to have the approval of my family.

way of assuring approval. The reality of my imperfection with dyslexia came first and seemed to lay the groundwork for shame and guilt about being human. Now imperfection was right up in front of my face and there was no way to deny it. I thought this was more than anyone should have to go through. I had to wear a three-eighths-of-an-inch lift on my shoe. In addition, at age fourteen, I thought that *everyone* noticed. And I knew that they were either feeling sorry for me or, mostly, mocking me.

I had no range of motion. I would never again be able to do the activities I used to do. No running, not even to the phone. No horseback riding. No carrying heavy packages. No springboard diving or any other high-impact sport. No driving a car with standard transmission. No walking long distances because of the fatigue. This was *not* fair.

To keep my sanity, I found I needed to focus on what I *could* do because the list of losses was so long. I could swim, walk short distances or sit for short periods of time. I was discovering that pain would remain with me for a lifetime. I feared I would always have a grotesque limp. There were so many fears I held inside. The bone would continue to deteriorate, which in the future would require additional surgeries. Because of the weight, I would only be able to have two pregnancies. I would not be allowed to even adopt a third child as carrying a third child would be too much weight on the hip. I was completely overwhelmed by these restrictions and losses. I could feel the emotional pain and it was numb at the same time. Grief would shoot through me and leave me empty and scared.

I continued to rock myself to sleep at night to help with pain tolerance. The movement attracted my attention away from the pain. Who would want to marry someone who moved around in the bed all night? Who would ever want to marry me with all these restrictions and problems? I thought that my value was in appearance and productivity and based on that belief I was a complete failure. I did not know how to cope with this and so I used much energy to stuff the pain down. Stuffing just caused more pain and I was in a repeating circle.

Remaining thin would help me to postpone the inevitable future surgery. My life became focused on how I could preserve the hip that I had in order to delay any future surgeries for as long as I could. Maybe by the time I needed surgery, medicine would have developed something more helpful, like a miracle cure.

My dad liked to go bird hunting with the help of his bird dog, Charlie. For target practice, he used clay pigeons at the shooting range. He kept his clay pigeons stored in boxes in our attic. The attic was the unfinished third floor of our home. The entrance to the attic staircase looked like just another closet in the upstairs hallway. I would disappear behind the door closing and locking it from the inside and ascend to my private sanctuary. I would often go up there when I was angry or sad and throw the clay pigeons with intense energy across the room, smashing them into the walls of the opposite side of the attic. I smashed and smashed until I no longer needed to. I would cry my heart out up there, praying to God the Father that He would have mercy on me and make everything better. God was my friend. In my childlike faith I trusted He had formed me in my mother's womb, had a plan for my life, would provide intervention and loved me just the way I was. He was the only one I did trust completely.

Somehow, I did feel better, even though things did not change. I believed God is a loving father, a protector who would intervene on my behalf and had an overall plan for my life. In the quietness of the attic, I had long talks with God. In my childlike faith, I trusted him with my life and everything that was happening to me. I believed God had a meaning and a purpose for my life and all that I was going through. I just did not understand what that meaning was. I cannot say how or when I came to know this. I did attend Sunday school. My mother had a faith that did she not question, she just believed. Even if I was taught about God's love, I had to accept it for myself. I prayed for wisdom to understand, patience to wait and persistence to endure until my life was relieved of the emotional and physical pain. I knew He saw my heart. I guarded my heart from others out of fear of being hurt by them. Too many experiences had already proven to me this truth. I could not endure more pain.

I developed a fear of falling, as it might lead to me hurting myself. I had been bold in most of the physical activities I did before hip surgery, so this new fear was such a stranger to me. My friends were in the stage of "no fear." They were not leaving me out, but they went places I would not. Isolation was a common and familiar feeling for me.

Sadness and grief at the loss of my lifestyle weighed heavily on my shoulders. There were too many feelings all jumbled up in my heart and mind to form into words, which themselves could be a jumble. The feeling that I had been made this way and that there was no way out of this situation overwhelmed me. When would it ever end? Now fourteen, I was developmentally more mature than at age ten. Because I had found a safe place to let out some of my frustrations, suicide was not a consideration anymore. The blessings of the faith that had been born in my heart provided a relationship for me with God the Father, who sustained me. I had surrendered my trust to Him because I believed He loved and cared for me. I felt confident He heard every conversation that we had. I did not feel inadequate when I talked with Him. The conversations seemed natural and I could tell Him anything. I could admit my failures and how I felt about others. God nurtured me as a parent would. I knew He was one who wasn't judging me. I believed that He loved me with all my flaws. I did not have to put my feelings into words. I just knew that He knew what I was trying to convey. When I did put my thoughts and feelings into words, they did not have to make sense for Him to understand. Sometimes my words would get all jumbled and come out in a way that confused others about what I was saying. Dyslexia would raise its prickly head and cause a sharp pain when talking to other people. But not with God. He understood. I was also blessed with two very close friends who would listen to me and provide guidance. They would hold my brokenness in their confidence.

Luke, my cousin, was a special friend. I did not know how to live with the pain, the altered lifestyle and the limitations I faced.

I did not know how to cope with the uselessness or the embarrassment I felt. Luke was extremely popular and had been on the football team when his life was suddenly changed forever. Polio left him paralyzed from the waist down. I went to him for counsel. His love and compassion for me in itself was healing. We talked about the continued usefulness of ourselves even with our physical limitations. Luke encouraged me to embrace the pain, as it was a sign that I was alive. He suggested that I go out and do something for someone else when I hurt and that the pain would lessen or maybe even go away for a short time. He said that focusing on the pain and all of the losses tended to increase the pain and the feeling of uselessness.

Luke's wisdom proved to be true. I began to develop a life of giving to others in service. It was not easy. Doing something for others meant that I had to forget about myself. As I struggled with this new style of coping with the physical pain, I found it easy to accomplish. But in the emotional pain associated with all the losses, I was not successful. The only way that I could cope with the emotional pain was to continue denying the truth that I was hurting or that I felt unworthy. My private self and my public self were becoming well-defined and they were not necessarily congruent with one another.

Anne was my childhood best friend. She lived next door to me. She knew about my Dad and my pain but she did not know how I felt about myself. We could talk about everything else. She was able to listen and show compassion yet never give unasked-for advice. Mother would go behind my back and talk to Anne to see if she could convince me to do something she wanted. Anne would always be honest with me about what Mother had said behind my back. I trusted her.

A month off crutches passed before physical therapy was prescribed. Because of the limited range of motion I had as the result of the damage and the inactivity for the last eight months, the physical therapist and I had our work cut out for us. Rehabilitating my muscles was a challenge. Everything was so tight. I had lost range of motion and the ability to move the leg with a smooth rhythm. In order to loosen the tightened muscles before exercises began, hot packs were placed on my hip for a while. Then the physical therapist and her assistant would stretch the leg. It hurt beyond my ability to tolerate the pain. I would either cry or get very angry.

One day, filled with anger and self-pity, I planted my heels in resistance and refused to work. Because I was hurting and feeling sorry for myself, I kicked the therapist as she was trying to help me.

I will forever be grateful to that wise woman. She said, "Let me show you something, *dearie!*" She whizzed open the curtain that separated me from the next person, and there was a little four-year-old girl. She had been born without any hip sockets and had already had three surgeries to build new sockets. The little girl was asked to get up and show me how well she could walk. She was so happy about life. Her face was animated, and she had the wonder of exploration in her eyes.

As I saw her struggle to walk even with her dramatic limp, I burst into tears. I found a deep sense of compassion for that little girl. It is eye-opening to see others whose struggles are greater than yours and there is nothing more powerful to help put things into proper perspective. I pleaded with God for a sense of joy in my life. I saw that self-pity and anger were destroying me. God was faithful and the anger melted for a time. The little girl helped me to see that coping and a change in perspective would make a difference. God was my friend and helper and I went to Him for help in changing my heart.

I had a difficult time actually getting to my right foot. Putting on my socks was tricky. I was unable to get my foot to rest on the opposite knee. Therefore, I had to rest the foot on the seat of a chair and put the sock on from behind. It was almost impossible to clip my toenails. Then there was the struggle to put on pantyhose so that my heel was in the correct place. I eventually learned to adapt and successfully accomplish these tasks. I learned that if I put my right foot or leg into whatever I was putting on before my left, then it was easier to get dressed.

Learning to walk again was hard work. I had to push through the pain and discomfort. Mother worked with me every day to help me with the home exercise program that the physical therapist designed. I could not do the exercises by myself and depended upon her help. I learned a heightened sense of self-discipline and persistence. The harder I worked, the more success I had. I learned to focus on the end result rather than the twisted physical image that I saw. For survival, I continued to deny that I actually hurt. I learned that if I focused on others and their needs, I did not have to face my pain and I would hurt less. I lost touch with the reality that I had needs, too. I projected my need for comfort onto helping others in their time of pain. I learned to minimize, if I could not deny, the degree of both physical and emotional pain. I learned to keep quiet about the degree of pain that I had because, if I did not actually put it into words, then I did not have to face the reality of the degree of suffering that I was having on any particular day. I didn't want to accept the pain by acknowledging it. But not acknowledging it didn't make it go away. I maintained a running dialogue with God, asking Him to bestow upon me the ability to endure. These conversations allowed me to remember that God had a plan for me. It helped me to stay focused on His promise that He would deliver me from my trials. It sustained my belief that God loved me.

Chapter 6

High School

*Nothing builds self-esteem and
self-confidence like accomplishment.*

—THOMAS CARLYLE

Because of my academic struggles and my health situation during the eighth and ninth grades, my teachers advised that I repeat the ninth grade. I was mortified! What a blow to the little self-esteem I had left. I would not even be able to graduate with my classmates. I now faced one more disappointment enveloped with public shame.

Dad came to the rescue by talking with me and suggesting that I possibly could go away to school, thus postponing anyone knowing what grade I was actually in. He had gone to a military high school after he had graduated from high school thus repeating his last two years. His way of talking with me affirmed that I was acceptable as I was and that I was not a failure for repeating. That was the wonderful dad of which I yearned to have more.

Mother and Dad were able to find a special high school for me to attend, but it was out of town. They made the sacrifice to allow me to be a boarder, returning home on holidays and in the summer. I was apprehensive about living away from home. I did not know what to expect in my new environment.

My academic salvation began when I indeed went away (1962) to an all-girls' school. I could postpone anyone knowing that I was repeating ninth grade and I could attend a regular school. Hockaday was not like the other private school that I had attended when I was ten. Hockaday is a regular private school, first through twelfth grades, that just happened to be in the beginning phase of a pilot program using the Gillingham method to teach dyslexic students to read.

At Hockaday, I met daily with my private tutor for four years. The tutoring session was only one hour a day out of the regular school curriculum. I could disappear into her class and none of the other students were aware of where I had gone. My disability went unnoticed. What a joy that was! In her classroom, we repeated the same lessons over and over. I relearned all the letters and sounds of the alphabet. I wrote them in the air, wrote them on the blackboard, wrote them on a piece of notebook paper, closed my eyes and wrote them as I pictured them. I said them out loud each time I drew them. I learned pronouns, verbs, prefixes and suffixes and whole words the same way I was learning phonics until it was second nature for me. In the tutor's room, it did not matter if I made a mistake. I knew she wanted to help me. I knew she believed in me. In addition, I believed that she knew I could learn to read. The high school blackboard experience became a healing ritual as I wrote the words down. I was encouraged and affirmed for the times I successfully accomplished the correct spelling of the words. I was never embarrassed or humiliated for making a mistake. There's no room for humiliation in education.

I was not allowed to read for myself during the first school year. I was read to, and all of my tests were verbal. This gave my brain time to recapture the early stages of processing sounds and letters. Glenda, another boarding student, had agreed to read all of my lessons to me aloud. Most of the tests in the high school were essay in form. The year I was not allowed to read, I was also not allowed to take written tests in any subject. Either I knew the answers or I did not. There was no way to try to finesse the answer when I had to take the test verbally.

> *The high school blackboard experience became a healing ritual as I wrote the words down.*

By the end of the first year, I was allowed to read for myself again. Once I was able to read and write for myself, I felt like there was more hope for actually succeeding and I was able to take the written tests. Each essay test was evaluated on content and grammar. I usually would get an A in content and an F in grammar. My grammar grades improved each year, and by the twelfth grade, I was passing.

Algebra and geometry were no problem. I excelled to the point I was allowed to teach the geometry classes when the teacher was away. I always made an A in math. I ran into difficulty in math when the problem was in written word form. Strangely, unless anxious, I was less likely to transpose numbers than letters. I was a natural at geometry. I saw in three-dimensions very easily.

It was a requirement to take a foreign language before graduation. I flunked French and Spanish. I could not hear the words, see the letters appropriately or pronounce back what I was hearing. I had difficulty enough with the rhythm of the English language, separating the phonemes, so it was no surprise that I couldn't understand a foreign language. Latin was the last choice. It was not a conversational language and therefore relieved some of the stress, as I only had to master the written word. I just had to memorize new vocabulary words, spell them correctly and, only occasionally, say them out loud. We spent most of the class time translating the Latin into English. This process was actually possible for me to accomplish and to earn a passing grade. Because so many of the English words are from Latin roots, I actually learned English far better than I would have imagined. My English grades went up; I began to make Cs instead of the usual D.

The teachers in school were encouraging and believed that I was capable of succeeding. They would give me positive feedback on a regular basis. My self-esteem began to bloom as I began to find ways to perform with academic success. I made As in math; Bs in history, science and Latin; and Cs in English.

I won an award for being named one of the favorite boarding students all four years of high school—an award that is given to students who exemplify leadership and moral character as defined by the founder of the school. I was elected to be president of my class in the boarding department in tenth-grade. I was elected to be president of the House Council my senior year. The House Council was to the boarding department as the Student Council was to the public school. To my amazement, many students looked up to me as a leader. This was different from my earlier years. I had been called *retard* and not many people wanted to be seen as the friend of a retard. There were other students at Hockaday who had dyslexia and we were all treated with respect and encouragement. I developed friendships while there that have lasted a lifetime. The value of a supportive and nurturing culture has never been more obvious to me.

Hockaday's gym had an Olympic-size swimming pool. I was allowed to swim laps every school day for four years. I had my daily reading tutor and my daily swim. I had specific daily land exercises to do, too. The swimming along with the exercises helped me to keep the muscles strong and to reduce the pain. Continuing to live in chronic pain remained a challenge to my ability to define myself as normal. But I was beginning to have more hope about life.

My self-esteem was growing due to the academic successes and the affirmation of classmates. However, living in pain, combined with how I saw my body image, continued to influence how I protected myself. Because I experienced some level of pain all the time, I chose to keep silent about my discomfort. I learned very quickly that people got tired of hearing me always talk about how much I hurt. The weather, too much physical exercise and unresolved emotions all increased the level of pain. I continued to minimize, deny and disconnect from the pain and the emotions that surfaced. I continued to emotionally withdraw from people at large. I would find a quiet isolated space when I was hurting; an attic away from the attic. I had learned all of those same skills as I learned to cope with having dyslexia. These were my survival skills, which allowed me the ability to function in everyday life.

I pretended I did not hurt and sometimes I succeeded in hiding the truth from others. Nevertheless, my close friends could see right through my pretense. For my public side, I maintained a smile and said that everything was fine. Inside, I might have been in agony.

As my self-esteem improved, I wanted to risk dating. I still had so many questions that remained about living with eternal pain, limited range of motion and a changed lifestyle. How would I cope? What are the consequences of taking medications to reduce the pain over a long period? What about complications? How many surgeries would be in my future? How many scars from the surgeries would mar my body more? Who would choose me for marriage with so many restrictions from the beginning? I could only have a limited number of children. I felt reasonably sure that there would be someone who would be happy with a family of four. However, the "but" did gnaw at me from time to time. Would I be able to develop a physically intimate relationship that would be satisfying to my husband as well as to me? Would sex hurt my hip? As a young teen, that was something that experience had not yet taught me.

I was not able to attend Sunday School as a boarder. We were, however, able to attend the worship service. I had memorized the Episcopal Liturgy, which could be repeated whenever I needed encouragement or even as prayer. I read scripture and prayed daily to find strength to keep going. I continued my intimate running dialogue with God, expressing my feelings about life and asking for His grace to endure. I was confident in His faithfulness.

I believed that, in time, the pains in my life would be resolved. I claimed many of Paul's sayings from the New Testament as sources of strength, which helped me to make some sense of my struggles. My favorite was "We have the mind of Christ" (1 Corinthians 2:16, RSV). That helped me regroup and clear the emotional confusion.

I was learning to focus on my new skills, which seemed to allow the dyslexia symptoms to subside. However, when anxious, stressed or fatigued, the symptoms would resurface. When feeling sadness, pain, discouragement, embarrassment, loneliness or anxiousness, the following scriptures brought me strength:

> "We know that in everything God works for good with those who love him, who are called according to his purpose. For those whom he foreknew he also predestined to be conformed to the image of his son, in order that he might be the first-born

> *among many. And those whom he predestined he also called; and those whom he called he also justified; and those whom he justified he also glorified."* (Romans 8:28-30, RSV)
>
> *"I can do all things in him who strengthens me"* (Philippians 4:13, RSV).

My mother encouraged me by stating that character was developed through hardships. She kept telling me I was becoming strong in nature and steadfast in courage. I accepted this life, for I wanted the strength of character; however, I did not want to hurt. Character is a major part of who I am as an individual. It is how I do what I do. It is why I do the things that I do.

> *"Suffering produces endurance, and endurance produces character, and character produces hope, and hope does not disappoint us, because God's love has been poured into our hearts through the Holy Spirit which is given to us."* (Romans 5:3-5, RSV)
>
> *"Many are the afflictions of the righteous, but the Lord delivers him out of them all."* (Psalm 34:19, RSV)

It is through suffering that I learn who I really am. However, there must be something that is present within me which enables me to push through the hardships without becoming and remaining bitter. Do I really know who I am until I face a hardship? If life is easy and goes along the way that I want it to, have I laid a foundation in my character that prepares me for success or losses? How do I resolve being wounded by others or even our hurting others? What responsibility to myself and to others do I have to face my true self and be transformed? What was transformation going to look like? I really had no idea. I just believed that God promised to transform me into the image of His son someday, somehow.

It is written that the Apostle Paul had a thorn in the flesh. I imagined it was a similar hip problem or even dyslexia. Paul had asked three times for his affliction to be removed, but God left it for a greater good. I could relate. My faith was steadfast in that God would also bring my suffering to a greater good. God the Father was the ultimate father I did not have. I loved my earthly father, but many times his words and his actions hurt me. God the Father never hurt me. He never abandoned me. I believe He never asked me to do more than the two of us could do together. He was the planner and creator of my life. He had formed me in my mother's womb and then had placed me in a family to provide the care and the resources I needed. He was intimately involved in what happened to me because He loved me. He answered prayers. He could see my heart. I yearned to know more about Him.

My faith was actually the glue that held me together and gave me a sense of identity. I had a reason for why all the pain had happened. I had a source of strength to pull from when I had nothing left. I had a reason to believe in life.

I enjoyed reading the Bible. I also enjoyed reading the writings of Kahlil Gibran. I could get lost in the mystery in his written words.

Because I was raised with music in the home, it was natural for me to listen to classical music when my nerves were stressed. Classical music brought me into a peaceful space. The dormitory was noisy and the music was a balm to the ears. I loved art; I could lose time looking at works by the masters. I loved visiting the museums to see the paintings of the old masters. I yearned to have their ability to express my emotions.

With the help of academic achievement, the strengthening of my muscles, which actually reduced the visible limp, and the development of good friends, I was beginning to come out of the hole I felt I had fallen into. I was able to begin to look for value in myself that I had not discovered before. I was beginning to entertain the idea that I just might be of value to myself and to someone else. How I saw myself and how I felt about my achievements were changing.

The day of graduation (1966) was a monumental emotional high for my family and for me. My cousin Adam was there and cried for joy. He had always been a loyal supporter of me and I had not known it. I had succeeded in hurdling the reading disability. I had begun to trust my judgments. I had begun to believe in my intelligence. I had increased in wisdom about life. I had matured in my faith and my understanding of God. I had learned that, with my persistent efforts and God's help, all things could be accomplished.

I was accepted into Endicott Junior College where I could specialize in fashion design. I had begun to believe I had talent, and I would have the opportunity to use my skills there without all the other superfluous academic classes. I had designed and sewn many of my own clothes. I had designed and made dresses for my close friends as graduation presents. Their presents actually fit and they were able to wear them. I had designed and made a formal dress, which I wore in a debutante pageant my junior year.

Most of the classes that I took in junior college were art-related. Fashion Design was like playing paper dolls again. We created little patterns and made them in the fabric of choice. To my surprise, I sailed through academically. One day in my drawing class, we were to present our drawings to the class. When it was my turn, the professor took my sketch, with a charcoal stick drew a line down the middle, and held it up for the class. His explanation was that the right side had form and the left side did, too, but the picture as a whole was out of proportion. He proceeded to explain to the class that I had dyslexia and my brain worked in conflict with itself. One of my eyes saw the left side of things and the other the right side. As a whole picture, the drawing was unbalanced. He asked the class to look closely so they would not forget what a drawing would look like by someone who had dyslexia. If the professor wanted to teach on dyslexia, he could have referred to drawings by Leonardo da Vinci, who also has been reported to be dyslexic, not to me!

I was beyond mortified. Where did he get that knowledge? Had he deliberately looked in the students' files to find something that he could use to humiliate me? I had thought, and had hoped, all that was behind me. I wanted to scream at the top of my lungs long enough to let out all the rage and the humiliation that welled up in my heart. Instead, I was able to hold it together until the class was over.

I did not take the negative critique as I had in the past, with silence. I went directly to the Dean and stated my case. At the next class, the professor apologized to me. The Dean had required the professor to give me a passing grade without requiring me to finish the semester. I was almost glad that had happened. I was able to realize I was developing boundaries appropriate to guard my self-esteem.

Chapter 7

Two Blind Dates

It's not about getting over things, it's about making room for them.
It's about painting the picture with contrast.

—BRIANNA WIEST

During the summers of high school and into college, we would have spectacular parties in our home. There were a number of popular local bands and we would book them to come and play. Martha and I could plan the menu with endless amounts of food. Mother's only requirement was that she was particular about who she wanted us to invite.

We would make the list of her "acceptable" girls and guys. Then I would have to pair them together. So many of my friends were involved in steady relationships. That was against Mother's rules—no going steady with just one young man. It was awkward for some of my friends because their boyfriend or girlfriend may not be on Mother's approved list. Couples were put together and invited to the party that way. If the young man did not want to bring the girl listed on the invitation, he could decline to come to the party. Getting past that strangeness, the parties were always a big success.

Mother wanted us to date many different kinds of men. If we dated just one young man, she believed we would not be able to make an informed choice regarding a marriage partner. I did sneak behind her back while I was away at school and had one steady boyfriend. As we matured, we realized the value of dating others. We dated for over two years before we decided to stop dating each other. While at home in the summers, I honored her request to date a variety of young men. My friends were helpful by setting me up with blind dates during the summers.

The summer between my freshman and sophomore years in college, I was asked to go on a blind date with a friend of a coworker from my summer job. The plan was to go in separate cars and all meet for dinner.

After he picked me up, he said he had forgotten something at his apartment and he needed to go back to get it before we met the other couple at the restaurant. He invited me into the apartment while he went to get what he had forgotten. I should have waited in the hot car, but because my friend had known him and had recommended him, I assumed that he was a safe date.

At first, he treated me as though I was a pretty young woman. I did not sense that my limp bothered him. I did not feel inadequate or shy. I felt confident and in control of my life. After a few minutes in the apartment, he forced himself on me. It happened so fast that I could not defend myself. All I could think of was that it was my fault, as I should not have gone into the apartment. I did not even think about screaming or clawing my way to freedom. I felt paralyzed and unable to take charge to bring about a different outcome.

I kept saying, "Stop," but it had no effect. He just became more forceful, holding me down with his hands and legs. Sexually, it hurt, and I was forced to be in positions that were compromising to my hip. My leg was in excruciating pain and I felt like it was being ripped out of my hip socket. Time seemed to stand still. I did not think the pain would ever end. I began sobbing and pleaded with him to stop, but he just kept on until he was finished.

> *It happened so fast that I could not defend myself.*

When it was all over, he told me to get up, clean up and we would go to dinner. I was shocked that he was so nonchalant about the devastating event that had just happened to me. I was bruised, bleeding, shamed and disoriented beyond my ability to process.

Like a robot, I did what he said and attempted to clean up. However, my body felt so dirty. The world was swirling around me and I was not sure that I was going to be able to stand. I felt sick to my stomach. My mouth began to gush with saliva and I was not sure I could get to the bathroom quickly enough before throwing up.

After emptying the contents of my stomach, I was overcome with tears. My tears kept pouring out, and just about the time I thought that I had control, the tears started falling again. My make-up was all over my face and my hair was a mess. I struggled to find any coping skill that would allow me to "act as if it had not happened." I had gone into his apartment of my free choice, but I did not ask to be raped. I had not been flirtatious, nor was I dressed in a loose fashion. What happened?

My old coping skills slowly began to assist me so that I could minimize, deny and disconnect from the pain. I think that I really was more in shock and therefore numb, rather than being successful with faking it. I was so traumatized that I went to dinner as planned. I did not even think of getting a cab and going right home. During dinner, I was miserable sitting next to the man who had just raped me. My friend noticed that something was wrong with me and asked about it. I was too full of shame to admit to her what had happened and to talk about it. I was able to ask the friend to take me home after dinner.

I stuffed the guilt and dirtiness I felt. Before the rape, I had begun to repair my self-esteem. Through education, physical therapy and some successes, I began to accept that I had some value. Because of this sense of worth, I was able to challenge the college professor who humiliated me in front of the art class. However, all of this crumbled as the result of the rape. The agony of shame returned as I wondered if I was responsible for the entire experience.

A few months after the rape, a high school classmate asked me to go on a blind date with one of her longtime friends who was on leave from the army. Why I went I do not know. Maybe it was because I had known my friend for a long time or because I felt motivated not to allow myself to be put in that same situation ever again. Maybe I needed to reestablish control over my life. I now knew to be on the watch for sexual advances.

I was rather apprehensive as I saw his car drive up to the curb. I wasn't sure this blind date was a good idea. What if the same scenario were to occur? What can I do this time to protect myself? Just as he opened the car door to step out, the skies opened up and let loose of a sea of water. He ran for the front door. He was drenched nonetheless. When I opened the front door to meet David, he was sopping wet. The water was dripping off his eyelids and running down his face. He looked at me with the silliest expression, and he had a sense of humility about his being wet. I looked into those big blue eyes, and I fell head over heels for him.

A dozen red roses came from him the next day with a note that read, "I enjoyed our time together. When can we have another date?"

David and I dated for several months, getting to know one another with comfort and compatibility. He had had polio as a child, and he had encountered his own struggles on his way back to health. I felt we understood each other. It seemed that David accepted me with all of my limitations. He was funny and outgoing. He had an energy about life that I enjoyed being around. I became spellbound by him and I daydreamed about spending the rest of my life with him. I know I fell in love with him with a passion as big as Texas.

As his family began to feel comfortable around me, they shared more and more about their family life. His mother, Sarah, shared her agonies in having a child with polio and the paralysis her son might face. She had worked very hard in their home exercise program to enable him to walk again. As she described how she put hot packs on his legs before all the stretching exercises, I remembered my own rehabilitation in learning to walk again. I felt at home with his family. Sarah also shared how wonderful the doctor had been through her son's illness. She stated that the doctor was the same one who had delivered both of her sons.

When Sarah called the doctor by name, something in the memory banks of my mind rang a loud bell. She was talking about the husband of my first-grade teacher! When I said to her that I thought that his wife had been my first-grade teacher, Sarah said his wife had gone back to teaching a few months after the doctor's premature death. No wonder my teacher had such difficulty with me. Her skills were rusty and she was grieving her losses. My scars were not completely healed, but this knowledge did give me an understanding into the fact that I was not the problem. Her losses and her ability to process her losses were.

How strange that I would date someone from a town close to mine whose pediatrician was the husband of my first-grade teacher! As an adult I could empathize with her situation and, at the same time, the memory of my first grade left a distasteful tinge in my mouth. A memory I felt I needed to stuff. I remembered the fear of ridicule, fear of rejection, fear of being found out and fear of failure. Somehow I still felt it was my fault.

David and I had been dating long enough for me to feel confident in our relationship, so I decided to risk sharing my date rape experience with him. I had a sense that if I did not tell him, I would be founding our relationship on withheld information and the strength of a solid marriage lay in open communication. My family had too many secrets to be a healthy family. I had also used the camouflage of silence to protect my emotions. I felt it was time to risk developing this new relationship on truth and openness.

I had not told anyone and it was a huge risk for me to be telling it at all. As I shared the story with him, it was as if I was experiencing the date rape all over again. I was sick to my stomach and my hands were sweaty. My heart was racing, which led to a mild form of hyperventilation. My mouth became dry. I felt like my throat was going to close before I could share the experience.

I told him how I had felt violated. I described the lingering guilt. I explained how I did not believe that I had asked for the sexual encounter. I felt that I had tried to stop it but that he had been stronger than I was. I talked about the shame I carried in my heart and how dirty I felt. I was at the point of tears from reliving the story as I told it to him. He could see I was in excruciating agony. In a heartfelt response, he put his hand on my shoulder to comfort me. I finished and waited. The wait seemed so long. After he heard my story, he turned his head away from me and was silent for a long while.

Then David said, "I forgive you."

I was confused because I could not process what on earth did I need to be forgiven for. I had been the victim and it was not my fault. As was my habit when my emotions were unable to process, I stuffed the pain. I discounted, I minimized and repressed what I actually needed to feel. I continued to date this otherwise wonderful young man.

CHAPTER 8

THE LIGHT OF LIFE

In order for the light to shine so brightly, darkness must be present.
—FRANCIS BACON

We dated only a short time before he asked me to marry him. I joyfully said yes. David and I married in 1968 on Easter Sunday, just shy of a year after the date rape. I stood at the altar in the Episcopal church and promised before God, friends and family to stay married for better or worse until "death do us part." This was a serious commitment of my heart. I planned to live happily ever after.

A few months after we were married, David received orders to report for duty in Vietnam. He was already in the military stationed at Fort Hood. The year was stressful for both of us.

I spent most of the year that David and I were apart with my parents. I noticed that I was beginning to develop a new ability to talk with them. Dad had been in World War II and he had the words I needed to hear. I began to understand many of the issues that they faced as a couple. My eyes were opened as I began to know my parents for who they were as people separate from their role as parents.

David returned safely from Vietnam and we started our marriage all over again. I took my role as a wife seriously. I really did not have extensive experience in relationship building. I thought that I was supposed to put my needs aside to care for him. After his return, I noticed there was something different in the quality of our relationship. I could not put my finger on it at the time. It seemed that he was overprotective of me. I sensed that he was not listening to me talk to him anymore. I did not understand what was happening and he would not talk about it.

One month after he returned, we were talking about some more of the fears I had developed from having dyslexia. He told me that he felt I was overexaggerating the situation and that I just needed to get over it. I was hurt and, feeling emotionally unsafe, I shut down. I was in the second most intimate relationship in my life, following that with my parents, and I felt that my reality was not being validated. I was not emotionally mature enough to challenge his response; I reverted to my old behavior patterns of emotional isolation. I decided I had been mistaken about being able to share openly with him. I thought that he had been empathetic before we married. Had I been blind in love? Did he change?

I gave only a portion of my life to him from that day forward. I was in conflict because I loved him deeply and now was disappointed. How could I hold these two opposite feelings at the same time? Love was stronger so I stuffed the disappointment. I set out to learn how to be a wife and to honor David as I had promised. We were married two-and-a-half years when Andrew, our first child, arrived in 1970. He was so cute! We wanted another child as soon as I was healthy enough to become pregnant again.

My second pregnancy had complications. The doctor suggested bed rest lasting about six months due to my threatening to miscarry. Ruth arrived eight weeks premature in 1972, weighing only four-and-one-half pounds. The first seventy-two hours were a crisis for all of us. The pediatrician was not sure Ruth would survive. I did not know if I could face the loss of her death. I cried buckets. Fortunately, the only complication she experienced was that she lost weight. She needed to stay in the hospital for a month to gain strength and to regain the weight that she had lost. The day I brought her home was a day to be celebrated. I took all of my clothes out of one of my dresser drawers and used it for her baby bed as she was too small for hers. I cut Pampers in half to fit her. I bought doll clothes, as there were no clothes for premature babies in the stores. Because of the trauma of her first few weeks, I feel I probably over protected her during the course of her life.

Soon after her birth, I developed complications from having endometriosis, which the doctor said would require a hysterectomy to correct. I knew that I was not supposed to have any more children. However, the fact that now my body physically could not, rather than my decision not to, presented an unexpected adjustment for me.

When I woke from surgery, my mother-in-law was standing over me saying that I must be a sinner; otherwise, God would not be punishing me with the need to have had a hysterectomy. Her faith was steeped in guilt. I had not been raised this way. I believed in a loving and forgiving God. I was aghast that Sarah would say such a thing, much less believe it. The God I loved would never have punished me this way. I believed my health was the result of all the extra x-rays from the hip and not punishment. David and I were discussing his mother's words and my belief in God, to which his response was, "Well, *you* did have sex as a teenager. I have read that early sex causes endometriosis to develop." I had no idea to what medical study he was referring.

I could only think that he was referring to the date rape. I did not know what was in his mind. I did not ask, as I did not want to know the answer. If he had held an attitude of disgust for me all those years because I had been raped, I did not want to know. It would mean that I would have to process it with him and I was scared of what he might say. So, I said nothing. I buried it as far down into my subconscious as I could.

After I returned home from the hospital, one of my next-door neighbors asked me: "So, how does it feel to be an it?" What a strange question. I was most certainly not an "it." I am a female as my chromosomes define; but now, what did it mean to be a woman?

Was it just the ability to have children? What was feminine? Was womanhood just a role that had been given to me by societal, religious or cultural norms? How was it or was it different from masculinity? Was my role to be married and have babies? Was my place to work only in the home? These are only roles. Womanhood certainly was more than having reproductive organs. Was there a different way for me to find the answer?

As I began my search to define what is womanhood and what definition of femininity would I claim as my own, I discovered the research endless. Narrowing it down to what is relevant here still leaves thought-provoking questions. Is womanhood defined by my accomplishments, my creativity, my nurturing as a mother or perhaps my values? Are there stages in which I develop womanhood? Am I a woman without being feminine? Is it dependent on how I look on the outside? Does my figure have to be a certain size? In one of my readings, the author describes the four functions of womanhood as the lover/companion, the mother/nurturer, the warrior and the mystic. But is function the essence of womanhood? The question remained for me to ponder for the next several years. I assume that women who are unable to conceive children or who have had a mastectomy

> *Is womanhood defined by my accomplishments, my creativity, my nurturing as a mother or perhaps my values?*

confront this same question. I was certain that I was more than my physique or its reproduction.

Within three months after the hysterectomy, the endometriosis had begun to grow back. This is not happening to me! My heart sank to the pit of my stomach. I was so disappointed. I could not cope with another surgery so soon after the hysterectomy; therefore the doctor put me on hormones in an attempt to shrink the infection. The medicine did keep the endometriosis from getting larger. I reached my limit in being able to tolerate the extra hormones. One day I was slamming cabinet doors, throwing things around the room and yelling at everyone. The children were crying because they thought I was angry with them. David did not know what to do, so he called the doctor. The doctor took me off the medicine at the risk of the endometriosis returning. The cost of my sanity outweighed the possibility of another future surgery.

Mother and Dad had begun to visit our home frequently. It warmed my heart to see them in the role of grandparents. I was able to observe them reaching out to my children with love. I was able to imagine how they had done the same with me, even though I was unable to feel it.

Within the year following female surgery, my hip socket had finally deteriorated to the point where a hip replacement was necessary. Tolerating the increased pain took most of my energy. My duties as a new mother and wife were being compromised. David's job took him offshore a week at a time, leaving me with the responsibility of our children. They were so young, Andrew three, and Ruth one-and-a-half, and I was almost a basket case with pain. It was out of the question for me to take pain pills as they made me sleepy.

The doctor prescribed an anti-inflammatory, which worked in the beginning, but I soon built up a tolerance even to the strongest dose. I sought consultation with three prestigious doctors at three different, well-known clinics across the country. I got three different opinions as to how their method of surgery would repair my hip. I chose the one that had the quickest recovery.

I went to Houston, Texas and had a total hip replacement (1974). The type of hip replacement I chose involved gluing the new hardware to my body. I would be able to walk within a few days post-surgery. The other procedures involved metal screws to bracket in the hardware and possibly bone grafts. With this procedure, I would be non-weight-bearing for six weeks to three months.

With the hardware glued in, the hip was strong enough to walk on immediately after surgery. My sister and her husband graciously invited me into their home in Houston for three weeks while I recovered. I had been advised to stay in the Houston area near the doctor. There had been cases in which the new hip implants had been rejected by the patient's body. These incidents were rare but the doctor wanted to take all precautions. Recovery was fast. The pain was almost gone. The horrible limp was almost nonexistent. For the first time in thirteen years, I was almost pain-free. The only limitation was that I could not perform impact sport activities.

Freedom! The legs were the same length. I threw away all of my shoes, because they had lifts built into them, and got new cute ones. I actually was able to wear sandals or walk barefooted. I could run toward my toddlers to save them if they went too close to the street. I could run for the phone. I had unlimited range of motion. Freedom, gratitude and joy were overwhelming emotions. It is so difficult to explain this new emotional high. I was now *normal*. I did not have the sense that I was physically retarded anymore. It was a miracle. The transitions I experienced as I learned to adapt to accepting all my losses had been such a struggle. The liberation was now breathtaking.

Even though I could have so many new possibilities in a new lifestyle, I chose to go on with my activities as before. I did add hiking and nature walks, but chose carefully, as this new hip had, at the time of surgery, only been proven for a thirteen-year life span. I wanted to preserve it for as long as I could. Revisions, I was told, might not be as successful. I was twenty-seven, and at thirteen-year intervals, I could have up to four or five more replacements in my lifetime.

Three months after recovering from hip surgery, David's job relocated him to Houston. A year later, a tumor was discovered in my body. As I was going through the tests to determine what it was, no doctor could rule out cancer. The doctor suspected endometriosis had grown back, but there was no guarantee that was true. Fear chilled my soul. I was just learning how to live free of pain. Why now? I felt it so unfair to have to stop again. If it were cancer, I might have pain again, have to face more loss or even die. Who would raise my children? If David remarried, would this step-mom love my children? Oh God, please do not let this be cancer. My life was just beginning to be full again. I had only just begun to feel *normal*. Why did I have to stop and endure another mishap? This was not fair! I had had enough!

I did not want to die. I was so scared I could not focus on the details of life. I was emotionally fighting off panic feelings that rushed over me. I found my emotions inside shaking like a seizure. Tears were an alternative to fright. Believing that everything was in God's hands was very difficult. This was a real crisis in my faith journey. For the first time in my life of faith, I began to question and I began to doubt.

Waiting first for the surgery, and then for the pathology report, seemed like an eternity. I had plenty of time to worry about the possible outcome. I actually made myself sick worrying about what was going to happen regardless of whether I worried or not. I was greatly relieved that the tumor was benign (1976). However, questions haunted me: Was the faith that I had leaned on and that which had sustained me a "Truth?" Would it sustain me beyond the grave? Was there an eternity? What had I done in my life worthy of showing to God? I had spent my life hiding the gifts and talent that He had given to me. I had denied that I was lovable. I had shied away from His leadings so many times. Would He forgive me?

I became an avid reader searching for something that would bring peace. Wayne Muller in his audiotape, *Touching the Divine*, defines spiritual work most poignantly. He states, "There are times in all of our lives when we are forced to reach deep into ourselves to feel the truth of our real nature. For each of us, there comes a moment when we can no longer live our lives by accident." He continues by stating "life throws us into questions that some of us refuse to ask until we are confronted by death or some tragedy in our lives." I could relate. He continued with more questions: "What do I know to be most deeply true? What do I love? Who do I believe myself to be? What have I placed on the center of the altar of my life? What will people find in the ashes of my incarnation when this is over? How shall I live my life knowing that I will die? What is my gift to the family of earth?" These were the same questions I was asking. He concluded by saying that "these questions come around and around like a spiral going ever deeper into the meaning of life." (Muller, 1994).

After listening to his audiotape, I entered into serious reflection, prayer, reading and discussions with people who might know and help me find the answers. I was not given an answer; I was asked a question that actually became the answer. I began to hear a call to give up my choices for my life. The calling got louder "to throw my life away and become an empty vessel for God to fill." A living death was the call I heard. Now, wait a minute. I feared death from cancer; but to consciously choose to die was a very different and very strange request.

The concept of giving up reminded me of all the times in my past when life's events or other people had dominated my soul. I resisted with all that was in me to retain control. I really did not know what my life was but it was all that was familiar. Even in all its pain and disappointments, the life I knew was less frightening than change. I was terrified of the unknown and the possibility of having to accept more sorrow in the new path. Jesus's example was loneliness, being misunderstood, betrayed, hardships, pain, suffering and being abandoned by both friends and God. I was tired of hurting physically and emotionally. His path also included love, commitment, selflessness, denial of self for the benefit of others and total forgiveness. Jesus knew who He was; He used his talents to the fulfillment of God. I did not see myself as any of those. I had buried my talents with fear and excuses, finding ways to avoid putting myself in positions to be ridiculed. I had built a magnificent wall to protect myself from emotional vulnerability. I had learned how to present a public side of myself and guard my internal side in secret. I felt so *unworthy* to respond to His calling.

My search ended in the middle of the night when I was awakened from a sound sleep by what felt like a bolt of lightning crashing into my chest. My body went into convulsions, shaking uncontrollably. Once awake, I heard a loud sound of the wind blowing violently. My first thought was the coming of the Holy Spirit at Pentecost. Was this God? The very same God of the entire universe? Was He right there in my bedroom? I felt an incredible fearful awe. I was not afraid of harm or destruction. I was, in a sense, in a state of holy reverence for the omnipotence and majesty of God. Who was I that He would come to have a personal meeting with me? My heart was racing so fast that my veins felt as though they were going to explode. I second-guessed the experience by saying to myself that maybe I was having a heart attack, and what I heard was only the blood rushing through my veins. I was beyond terrified. I thought if I hid under the covers, I would discover I was dreaming.

In truth, there is nowhere I could go to hide from God. I accepted the invitation to converse with God. I accepted the truth there was nowhere I could hide and He would not come and find me. I accepted that His choice of me was because it was His choice and there was nothing I had or would ever do to deserve His presence.

Then I heard His loud, yet gentle voice calling me again to give up my life and to follow Him. He was calling me to set aside my will for His. He was calling upon me to give up self-desire, self-decisions and self-direction. He was calling me to put aside my definition of myself and to be transformed by Him. He was calling me into death. I was so afraid of the unknown. I curled into a fetal position; my face down into my chest in the bed and squinted my eyes tightly shut.

Then, something mysterious happened. I found my eyes were open and I was no longer in the bed. I was somewhere else. I was standing in the middle of an empty landscape. It was void of anything familiar except a top (sky), light gray in color, and a bottom (land), a little-darker gray. I became even more aware as I realized God had always chosen me and He would hound me until I chose Him.

His question again, "Will you come and *follow* me?"

I panicked as I looked for a way to surrender to His invitation. I remembered that Jesus would by my guide, for he had gone before and knew the way. I yelled "Jesus" and stretched out my hand into the unknown, asking Him to show me the way. At the instant I felt my hand touch the hand of Jesus everything became a brilliant, pure white-radiating light. Pulsating from the center of the white light were rays of pure colors—red, blue, green, yellow, purple, orange—all of them. The brightness of the light did not hide its essence, for it was the risen Christ.

I knew without words being spoken that it was He. I felt as though I had been gone from my home for a very long time and now I was back where I belonged with Christ. He emitted from that brilliant white light, total acceptance and a pure holy love for me. I felt peace words cannot explain. I felt comfort. I felt connection. I felt embraced by a love that was indescribable. I felt secure. I was content. I was satisfied.

Our conversation was not dependent upon words. He conveyed that His sacrifice was necessary and sufficient. His life and death on earth flashed through my consciousness. It was like someone showing a video and reading the story simultaneously at the same instant. Time did not exist. Past, present and future were the same. Messages and insights were conveyed without words. I just knew. He is who He says He is! He will protect me. He would always go before me, showing me the way to live. His love for me was more comforting than snuggling in front of a fireplace. More peaceful than anything I have ever experienced. More beautiful than the most gorgeous of all sunsets. As real and yet as mysterious as the feel of the wind blowing across my face. Words seem to really take away from the wonder and depth of the encounter. Nevertheless, words are all that I have to try to describe the mysterious.

The next thing I knew, I was back in my own bedroom, sitting in an upright position on the edge of my bed. It took a few minutes for me to actually realize I was awake and back in my bedroom. I no longer heard the rushing of the wind or felt as if my blood was racing violently through my veins. Slowly, I could sense I was still filled with wonder and amazement.

Where had I gone? Had I actually died and gone to Heaven? I felt as though I had and had been resurrected. I was empty, and yet full. Empowered, yet humble. I was aware that I am a small speck in the universe and yet infinitely important to God. I was awed that there is a place other than this earth. I was surprised by the sense that I had returned home after being away for a long time. That must mean I had been there before and I knew it as home even if it were only in that I was in the mind of God before I was created. I was with God even then. I rested in peace through the remainder of the night. So much to process.

It was my present from God and I held it in secret.

I did not tell anyone; I was concerned I might be called psychotic. Another concern was that people would think I had made it up. The visitation was too awesome to be devalued as being made up. In addition, some of my neighbors believed that visions were of the devil. I did not want to share this beautiful experience with them. They would just make fun of it. It was my present from God and I held it in secret. I was not well-versed in the scriptures and could not quote verses with them to support my experience. In fact, I could not even prove that the vision was real.

The next day Martha came to visit me. She kept asking what new make-up I had bought. She said that I had an unusual glow about my face. She said I really looked at peace and she thought maybe I had had a face-lift! Her witness was what I needed to verify that my experience with the Holy One was more than a dream. I have never again seen such a brilliant, white light or felt so peaceful. Over the course of the rest of my life, my understanding of this experience and my relationship with God would change many times as it grew deeper and wider.

As time passed, I began to grieve having to be back here in this world. Like the disciples Peter and John, I wanted to pitch my tent on the mountaintop and live there forever. I longed to go back to wherever *it* was. I yearned to be with Jesus again. I no longer felt I fit here on earth. I had been enlightened and all of the rest of life was boring, cruel and a series of struggles. Soon, I began to understand that I was called to let go of all the old garbage and to replace it with truth and honest, open expressions about who I am. I was called to search my motives. I was called to be in alignment with the person that God originally had in mind when He formed me in my mother's womb.

I had built so many walls to protect me and now I was called to be vulnerable. I had made many choices based on what I wanted or what I was trying to avoid. Now He was calling me to hear only His voice and to respond. I was apprehensive. I had never walked this path before.

I found I was remembering people and places I had not thought of in a long time. I remembered the cousin, Luke, who had been such an inspiration to me when I was a teenager. I remembered that I had never told him how much his counsel had inspired me. I decided to call Luke and tell him. I got his phone number from my mother but found that I could not call him. My throat would close and I would begin to cry every time I contemplated making the call. So to relieve my stress and follow God's leading, I attempted to write a letter. I judged my words as insufficient and never sent any of the many letters that I had written.

A few weeks into this gentle nudging by the Holy Spirit, Mother called and invited us to come for the weekend. I gathered the kids and off we went. After we got there, Mother told me that Luke was at his ranch (his second home), just a few miles from her home, also for that same weekend. He had asked for all of us to come for dinner.

I knew that God, in His grace, was giving me another chance. I had been so concerned with how I would be perceived that I could not follow God's leading. However, there I was again, and His insistence was obvious. I prayed for courage and grace to verbally tell Luke at dinner. I prayed for an opportunity for us to be alone so that I would have time to speak from my heart. During the evening, God was faithful and did provide several opportunities for me to speak. Each time my throat would tighten and I would feel that if I spoke, I would not stop crying. I was experiencing an overwhelming sense of gratitude and love for Luke and I could not say those words. The evening ended and I had not been faithful to God nor honored the life of my cousin.

The following Monday, Mother called and said that Luke died early that morning. I felt so empty. God knew Luke needed to hear what I had to say. My brother did call Luke the night before he died. Chad had the same nudging and he had followed his calling. How could I understand my disobedience and all of my excuses? There was no undoing what I had done. How many times had I neglected to follow God's nudging because of all the petty reasons that I made up? How often had I not trusted that if God has called me to a task, He would give me the courage and resources to accomplish it? Listening to God and then following His instruction is a major part of walking in the friendship that He offers me. I found forgiveness but not until I had searched my soul and accepted responsibility for my fear.

The fall after I had my Christ experience, I enrolled in a university to pursue a degree in Christian Education. This seemed to be a way I could serve the Lord with the new insights that I had been given. It was a courageous step for me to enter into the academic world. I had no idea if I could but I wanted to try. My son was in first grade and my daughter was starting kindergarten, which for her was a half-day. My husband worked long hours and was not interested in helping me with any of my homemaking responsibilities so that I could attend classes or study. I asked for help but he kept saying that I needed to stay home and take care of the children. He was busy with work and he was tired when he got home. I lasted one semester. Because of his resistance to my dream and the fact that I could not accomplish everything on my own, I withdrew. I was disappointed but had no idea, until much later, just how angry I was. After that, without even realizing it, the marriage died in my heart. I remember losing the enthusiasm for the marriage and attending counseling. I began to talk with David about myself, my needs in the marriage and that I really was lonely. I began to tell him that I did not feel a union with him. I admitted I felt that our communication was less than satisfying. I shared I did not feel that he was listening to me. It had seemed to me that he always had something other than what I was saying on his mind. I wanted to talk about the changes in our relationship that had occurred after his tour in Vietnam. I wanted to talk about how we differed in child rearing.

I wanted to talk about how different we were becoming. I was honest about the dryness of our marriage and how I wanted either for things to change or for a divorce. I remember yearning for a divorce but choosing to stay both because of our children and because there were parts of the marriage that were good. We both enjoyed the outdoors, we enjoyed vacations, we visited our parents often and we enjoyed the same style of music. I loved his good nature and his positive outlook on life. His work ethic was noble. While coworkers would lie or cheat David would remain faithful to his code of ethics. Our communication was poor, our philosophy for child rearing had some definite differences and I questioned if the marriage was based on mutual respect for each other's personal growth even if the other did not agree. He was set in his ways and that made it difficult to hear my needs or the children's.

We began marriage therapy. There was just enough time to get the issues out in the open and then David was offered a new job in West Texas (1980). We had not had time to process our differences or the opportunity to find resolution. It was a good opportunity for him. I wonder now if the relocation was a diversion from the marital strain we were facing. David was so busy he didn't have time to think about the marriage. He invested his energies in the job to become the best he could be. I was proud of him for what he accomplished. I, on the other hand, was lonely.

Chapter 9

WHY HAS GOD FORSAKEN ME?

Doubt is as crucial to faith as darkness is to light. Without one, the other has no context and is meaningless. Faith is by definition, uncertainty. It is full of doubt steeped in risk. It is about the matters not of the known but of the unknown.

—CARTER HEYWARD

Life is kind when it gives us brief periods of rest before we've another hurdle to climb. Spiritually, the first year we moved to West Texas was good. It was on the heels of a life of hope, almost pain free and with a renewed faith. Little did I know I would be led into the darkest night of my soul, barely to come out alive. I really do mean *alive*.

All of our unresolved marital issues resurfaced with bold clarity. My coping skills were not sufficient to help me deal with what was ahead of me. My acceptance of my calling from God was about to be tested by fire and purified.

After David and I married, we both left our roots and became Presbyterian. We believed that it was important to raise our children in one faith. I was active in our new local church teaching Sunday School. I was one of the presenters in a four-state regional workshop. I later was nominated to serve as a deacon on the church's governing board.

My commitment to serve grew more easily than my ability to grow spiritually or psychologically. I was fearful of changing inside. It required that I change in my ability to communicate my deep wishes. I prayed all the time for help and guidance. I made a special attempt to hear the voice of God and respond. I vacillated between the courage to respond to God's leadings and resisting out of fear or lack of trust.

> *I was fearful of changing inside. It required that I change in my ability to communicate my deep wishes.*

One day I heard Him ask me to go to a church and give a particular woman a special message from Him. Her face, a picture of the church and the message flashed before me. I thought that, if I really did go and do this, others would think me bizarre. I had never met this woman.

After the nudging from God became stronger and I could no longer push Him away, I left the house to do what He was asking me to do. I drove around town and did not see the church.

"Great! I got out of this," I thought as I started home. I got out of that embarrassment. But, lo and behold, on the way home, there was the church. I circled the block many times before I got the courage to park. I sat in the car reassuring myself that God had sent me to do His work. I got out of the car and went into the church. As I entered the church building, a woman asked me why I was there and if could she help me.

I told her I had no idea why I was there. She told me I might find the answer in the sanctuary and pointed the way. I followed her instruction and found the sanctuary. Feeling like a complete fool, I knelt to pray. After praying, I got up to leave. But exiting from the room just across from the sanctuary walked the woman to whom I was supposed to give God's loving message. Tears rolling down her face, she walked toward me. I explained how I got there to the church and the message I was to give her; God heard her prayers and would honor them. He would bless her ministry. She had been praying with her prayer group for hours asking for answers to her prayers. She invited me to pray with them. This group became a help to me in the days ahead. I had a sense that my new friend and I had been blessed by a loving God. I was aware that what I had felt led to do was of God and that He had definitely been present in my life. Again, God was telling me that He was not out in the universe somewhere but involved in the very stuff that life on this planet is made of.

Because we had just moved to a new town, I had not had time to develop trusting friendships. Even though I had been asked to join her prayer group, I felt isolated. I was ashamed to admit I needed help. I was scared and unable to talk to my husband, so I returned to my facade of holding everything inside. David's new job had begun to take most of his attention away from our marriage and his time with our children. It seemed he had become more impatient with the children and more critical of me. He would scream at them with words I felt were damaging to their self-esteem. Remembering all the hurtful words that had been said to me, I hurt doubly. I withered under my own memories of childhood. I was unable to emotionally protect my own children from the same things that hurt me. His focus was his new job: how he was perceived, how he needed to change to fit in, his new duties and the new people. His new job was different from his other jobs in that it was a private company. He was hired to build a gas processing plant which proved to be a significant challenge for him. The pressures were demanding and the deadline for completion added yet another challenge. The company employees worked hard and partied just as hard. There was always a social gathering to attend. Heavy drinking in the evening; the remedies for hangovers were endless. Secrets were kept about the faithfulness of spouses. It was difficult for me to see other spouses in the daytime and to know what happened. I resented being put in this position of deception.

The company parties with their indiscriminate drinking, fake conversation and social climbing repulsed me. So did getting sitters for the children so we could attend those parties and company vacations. My husband needed these social interactions for his progression in his new career. I felt devalued and my needs rejected. Had I been in a different place in my life, I would have known that this was not a rejection of me. I would also have been able to verbalize my feelings and needs as a wife and mother. So many people might not have been ultimately hurt by my choices and actions. However, I was not in that other place. I was angry, alone and in agony. I felt abandoned.

The emotional pain level once again reached an equal magnitude to that of my bone problems. My body could not distinguish between physical and emotional pain. Both took on physical manifestations. To some degree, I had been able to talk about the physical pain; but having or expressing the emotional pain was not acceptable. Learned from my parents, these response patterns were necessary for my own survival.

To numb the pain, I began to drink. David was drinking, so I justified my drinking by thinking I would be able to hide what I drank. But something happened to me; I became a closet drunk. I drank until I was emotionally numb or passed out. Very quickly, I found myself trapped. I could not stop. David and I began to argue and we said so many hurtful words. It would have been kinder if I had been able to say what I had wanted to say to him in a sober state, even if those sober words hurt. But the drunken words cut like knives into both of our hearts.

Our children were caught in the middle. David taught them to be caretakers of their sick mother. My own family dynamics were mimicking that of my upbringing. I swore I would not do to my children what had happened to me, but there I was doing it. The imposed role of caretaking would haunt them for many years to come. It would destroy many of their own relationships into adulthood.

I grew up hating my father's drinking behaviors. I hated the fear I lived in, never knowing when he would become a monster. I hated watching him become verbally cruel and hurtful to my brother. I feared for Chad as he drove to bars late in the night looking for Dad to bring him safely home. I hated the embarrassment I felt when we were in public and Dad was drunk or verbally ugly due to his irritability. Moreover, I hated the changes in his otherwise wonderful personality. He was sometimes so funny and witty. He had incredible insight into people. I loved him deeply, and I think that is why my emotions were so intense. I was disappointed by love. I was angry with Mother for not protecting me. I think somewhere in my unconscious I blamed her for not fixing this problem.

Mother was a stoic and held everything in. Dad was hysterical when drinking. Mother's response to him was cold, and she shut him out from herself emotionally and physically. His addiction was never discussed with us. We did not know when we were young that Dad was an alcoholic. Silence about family situations is not always best. It would have been healthy for Mother to tell us that the problem belonged to Dad and that we did not own the problem. Martha, Chad and I carried the blame for Dad's behavior and felt personally responsible as young children do. We needed to be set free from this inappropriate responsibility. We experienced the effects of his addiction in mood swings and sometimes scary behaviors. I hated myself for becoming just like that which I hated in my father. To my horror, I found that my personality was changing, too. I swore I would never be like him, and there I was, becoming just like Dad. It seemed so strange that I became the thing that I hated most. Fortunately, it was that same hate that brought me out of my addictions. It gave me the motivation to struggle through therapy and, eventually, to become and to remain sober.

I began the search for sobriety. I went to a psychiatrist. He said I was still playing games and that I was not ready to be sober. His response was difficult for me to process. I had gone to him for help and I left his office confused as to why and how he came to that conclusion. I do not know why the psychiatrist chose this approach toward me. I needed help and I felt rejected, an issue that had plagued me for a long time. Wounded, I did not return to his office. I tried on my own to resist the temptation to drink. I remember many times being curled up in a fetal position in the corner of our bedroom, rocking back and forth, pleading with God for help. Many times a black, ghostly figure would manifest itself in front of me like a mirage. It seemed to have more power over me and I would eventually give in to drinking again.

My love for my family and my inability to stop drinking on my own power, plus desperation, led me to seek admission to a rehabilitation center. In that facility, I went through detoxification and an Alcoholics Anonymous twelve-step program, only to return home to the same problems. I saw the problem as a relationship problem because I thought it was rooted in my marriage. I knew there were things my husband needed to change. Taking responsibility for my own behavior was not what I wanted. I was still playing the blame others game. David saw my drinking problem as belonging solely to me. I had not yet developed the emotional maturity to understand I had the right to my feelings, opinions and choices. I did not have to change to please others, and I did not have to feel guilty that I felt the way I did. I had not developed the verbal skills to constructively express my needs. David refused to go to therapy with me; he thought it was my problem alone and, therefore, his presence in the therapy room was not needed. I needed the situation to change, but it was not changing. I needed his help. I was so angry.

I went back to drinking. This led me to choose another rehabilitation center. As I look back now, I believe I was waiting for David to change; then it would be easier for me to change. In retrospect, I was giving David responsibilities that were not his. It was my individual path to sobriety to walk. By placing the outcome of my sobriety on David, I set myself up for another failed attempt. I set myself up for failure.

There was a part of me that was determined to reach sobriety. I chose to enter the John DeFore Counseling Center. As I unpacked my bags and settled in to my multiroommate room, I was hopeful but mostly apprehensive. More drinking time had passed with many more heated arguments between my husband and me and more crazy driving with our children in the car. I was beginning to have memory blackouts. I needed this rehab to help me live a sober life.

The focus of the second rehab center was on the roots of my drinking and the behavior changes necessary to live a sober lifestyle. What was I running from? What was the pain? What was I afraid of? How was I projecting my problems onto others and holding them responsible for my lack of decisions or resolutions? Therapy began with the assignment to write my life story down with all its good, bad and ugly experiences. I had never written my story down. I found it difficult to write. For with each event, my awareness of the individual situation compounded the total. It really was an exceptionally painful journey to go within and face my monsters. I would get sick to my stomach as the memories surfaced and I looked them squarely in the face. As I grieved for both all the hurt I had experienced and all the hurt I had inflicted on others, I cried from a place that was deeper than I knew existed. The therapist and I identified the monsters that I needed to address in the two weeks we had together. Therapy time was scattered throughout the day; then writing assignments at night.

> *It really was an exceptionally painful journey to go within and face my monsters.*

I struggled to verbalize what was inside. I found that I had plenty of emotions but I was not in touch with the words to describe the emotions. Deep sorrow was the first emotion to surface after reading my story to my therapist. I had learned early to stuff my feelings, as I felt they showed my weaknesses and I needed to be in control. As I gradually faced reality, there was pain, for sure, and, eventually, peace and the lifting of a heavy burden. This surprised me.

After the initial telling of my story, therapy sessions shifted from my initial therapist to many different therapists, one at a time. Each therapist had an expertise in a certain area. As my story was multifaceted, I had different areas that needed addressing. My drinking behaviors were the first to be addressed. I had built walls to protect myself from my emotional and physical pain and letting those walls down created high levels of anxiety. Looking into the truth that I had avoided was agonizing. I was facing accountability in a sharp way. Therapy sessions explored the reasons, attitudes and behaviors associated with my drinking. On one particular day in therapy, the issues were getting too deep. I was fearful of facing the truth. I got up to run for the door to escape the pain.

The therapist said in a loud voice, "Go ahead and run. That is how you have handled everything in the past. Go ahead and *run!*"

I stood with my back to the therapist and with my hand on the doorknob, ready to make my escape. I began to scream at the top of my lungs and shake the doorknob violently. I knew that if I did run out the door, I would never be sober. Even though my emotions were screaming, my will held my hand frozen securely on the doorknob.

I choose not to run out the door. I returned to the chair and, with fear and trembling, committed to face the issues that had bound me to the devastating cycle of addiction. Truth seemed too painful to live by. I'd rather live in an illusion of protection to avoid the pain. The problem with this was that I also created a false image of myself. My therapist had me start a list of all the lies I told about my drinking. Then he widened the project to encompass accountability of all lies that I could think of, even lies I said about myself. It would take me the rest of the two weeks before I began to identify the lies I told to myself.

I was able to express my wounds from dyslexia. I was able to put into words how I saw myself with my limp and twisted body image. I was able to describe the negative criticism I had felt from my mother growing up. I was able to put into words my hatred for my dad's drinking behaviors. I was able to express my feeling of being unwanted by my birth mother. After much delving into my parents and my relationship with them, I was able to discover that they did the best they could and I actually admitted that I loved them deeply.

I identified some losses associated with the lifestyle resulting from my physical disability. I was thirteen when I lost most of the activities I loved. Preteen was a time when my body image and how others viewed me were critical. Self-consciousness played out in presenting a strong character, not because that is who I am but because I needed to camouflage how inadequate I really felt. With the loss of my familiar lifestyle came a confused identity. Who was I now? I needed to walk into the loss of identity and, with the help of the therapist, rebuild an awareness of the person I had become: all the new talents I had acquired and all the skills I had found to cope. I remember breaking out in uncontrollable laughter at myself as I thought about some of those skills, such as sewing, being a creative gardener or being a Sunday School teacher. In truth I did have major losses for someone so young, but those losses no longer had to define who I have come to be.

The idea of "abandonment" and the emotions and resulting behaviors associated with being adopted first became formed through the therapeutic process. I came to understand that deep within I believed there was something wrong with me; otherwise, I would not have been given up for adoption. I reached for the truth and came face to face with the idea that what I had believed was false and that the truth was to be discovered. I was ready to rewrite my belief system. Closely associated with abandonment is rejection. I remember in another session, the therapist challenged me to face how I felt when I was rejected. I attempted to make light of it and change the subject. However, he would not let me go there. My insides felt all twisted and I thought I was going to throw up. The more I stuffed the emotion the sicker my stomach felt. I struggled to find a way to go into those feelings. Yet, to feel rejection was for me to be rejected. I had to decide I wanted to be free more than I was afraid. I found myself sinking into my chair and beginning to sob until the sickness was out of my stomach. Another therapist helped me come to some sense of resolution about having been date raped. I had carried the burden that it was my fault. It was difficult for me to let this go. For so long I had assumed that everything that had happened to me was my fault. I should have known better, could have done better or it was my fault that I had been formed as I was from the beginning. Emotionally weary from the intense therapy that had already occurred, I thought I did not have the energy to resist facing the date rape. As the therapist's gentle way led me into the center of the rape, I felt like it was happening all over again. I felt violated and helpless. I felt trapped with no way out. I felt used, devalued and then discarded. My body's reaction was limp and lifeless. I did not have any energy to describe in words how I felt emotionally or physically. The therapist said, "What about the person who raped you? How do you feel about him?"

I opened my mouth and to my amazement the words came rolling out and did not stop until I ran out of words to describe my rage. What an insight. I was not only angry at the rapist, I was angry toward all the people whose actions and attitudes left me feeling violated, trapped, devalued, rejected, abandoned, ridiculed or unworthy. After two weeks of intense therapy, vitality for life returned.

Feeling "well," I returned home with determination to remain sober. I started to go to AA for continued healing and support. However, when I went to my first meeting, I saw too many people I knew. Pride sent me right out the back door. I realized quickly that not all of the buried issues were in fact healed. I had only touched the surface. I had identified some of the issues, but the lasting transformation that the change within required had not yet been formed. There was yet another layer of the unconscious that needed to surface.

Although I tried, I was unable to stop drinking using sheer will. Why could my own will not sustain me? With personal persistence and the help of a tutor I had pushed through dyslexia, learned to read and with the help of a physical therapist had learned to walk again. Both of these hurdles, while guided by educated professionals, would not have been attained if I had not done the work. I had assumed that my efforts would help me reach sobriety. The missing ingredient was someone supportive to guide me along the way. The person I needed to help me was my husband. I left the second rehab center still expecting him to walk with me through my journey to sobriety. He was not in agreement with me. With all the might in me, I could not find the strength to overcome my desire to drink. The roots were deeper than I could imagine. Without those roots being uprooted, exposed and healed, I was soon back into my old habits. I spiraled down into an even darker place. I felt that I was experiencing hell right here on earth.

The world became black and barren. I felt so isolated. I became empty of anything positive. I began to curse and blame my birth mother for conceiving me. I began to curse the environment in which I grew up. In addition, I began to curse God for abandoning me when I was crying out so desperately for healing. This was the first time in my life I had felt that God was not answering my prayers. I was experiencing my own personal "Job" story. I was full of rage that I was alive. I became consumed with fury that I was not able to be in control of the situation. I blamed my dad for the environment in which I grew up. I blamed him for teaching me the coping skill of drinking. I blamed God for abandoning me. Christ had come in the past but He was now nowhere to be found. Was I being left to suffer? This difficult place full of rage carried such an emotional intensity that it was about to consume my very life; and then, the very healing that I needed was born out of this very dark place.

I had wanted to know about my roots for as far back as I can remember. When I would ask my mother if she knew anything about my birthmother, she would only say that my birthmother was financially unable to take care of me and I did have an older sibling that was also given up for adoption. I needed to know but I was afraid to continue asking my mother. I did not want her to think I was ungrateful for being adopted. Now, in desperation, I began to search for my roots. I needed to know if alcoholism was in my family heritage. Every step of the way, I faced the fear of rejection, the fear that my needs would be denied and the fear that I might find something that was yet more painful and I would be unable to cope. I was surprised to discover the fear of rejection carried such a powerful influence over my choices and behaviors. I had no idea how it had guided my emotional responses to life situations. Because of fear I froze, avoided voicing myself or involving myself in activities where I might be rejected. For example, I refused to take piano lessons because the teacher would require that I be in her recital. I was able to see that I had strong emotional responses to not having my needs met. I felt fear but did not understand the magnitude at that time. I experienced only that fear as related to being adopted.

The first action that I took was to write the judge in the county who had issued my final adoption decree and asked that my records be opened. I said my reasons were because I was looking for medical information that might be genetic. For example: did my birth mother have dyslexia, bone problems, cancer, high blood pressure or something else?

The county clerk called me and said the judge did not grant that kind of request, but she would hand carry my letter to him and ask on my behalf. It was a wonderful surprise to open a letter from her and find a copy of my final adoption decree tucked neatly inside. I was again surprised by the document's contents. On the form were the names of my birth mother, Kate, and birth father, Steve. I discovered the name she had given to me at my birth was also on the document. Who was this other person recorded on the legal document? This new name presented yet another crisis to my identity. Who am I? I did not even like the original name. I was bonded to my name of Jeanne. This other name was foreign and intrusive into my life. Yet, it represented the first seven months of my life in a different world. What had been those experiences?

Next, I wrote the county in which I was born and asked for a birth certificate using my original name, Donna. I was issued a new certificate. This should have been a sealed document, but for some reason, I was sent a copy. I contacted the chamber of commerce in the town where I was born, according to the new birth certificate, under the pretense of completing a genealogical trace and asked for information about where the old newspapers were kept. The woman on the phone asked who I was looking for and I told her I was looking for Kate McCoy.

She stated, "I knew her. She used to have a blue-eyed baby girl with the prettiest brown curly hair. I wonder what ever happened to that baby. If you find out, please let me know."

My throat closed up, and I could not speak. I wanted to shout, *"That's me!"* but an overwhelming fear bound my throat closed. As suddenly as my throat closed, it opened, and I was able to say, "That is me. I am looking for Kate." She told me she knew where some of Kate's family members lived and she would call them to ask about Kate's whereabouts. She stated she also had an adopted daughter. She continued by stating she was trying to help her daughter locate her birth mother. She understood what I was going through. I believe she answered the phone that day as a blessing from heaven.

When she called back, she told me Kate had died a few years before but some of the relatives were willing to talk to me. She apologized for having to tell me the disappointing news and wished me well in the continuation of my search to find other family members.

I wept. I was so sad. Why had the search ended with me finding my birth mother but not being able to talk to her? I had so many questions that now will never be answered. All the doors to find Kate had opened miraculously, as though the information was meant to find its way to me. Yet, it had led to a dead end. Why did it have to turn out this way? My need to talk to Kate could not ever be met. There was an empty space where I needed her to be. As I experienced that empty place, I became aware that I had always restlessly searched for a way to fill it.

After I had some time to sort through these emotions, I called the relatives, Seth and Roda. They told me I had an older half-sister, Nancy, who had also been given up for adoption, two younger half-sisters, Karen and Susanna, and two younger half-brothers, Pete and Mark. The relatives knew where Nancy lived and gave me her number. They did not know where the other siblings lived.

I called Nancy. It is so strange to call a perfect stranger and announce that I was her sister. Bless Nancy; she took it in stride. I went to her home to meet her, and discovered that we are very much alike. She is gifted in playing the piano and in singing. She loves to sew and loves nature and traveling. She shared her open adoption story with me. She described her visiting Kate several times throughout her life. She described the other siblings, for she had also met them. When I had talked on the phone to the relatives, they had told me that Kate's doctor delivered me at her home. Nancy knew the house where our birth mother had lived, so she took me there. The home looked like it had been abandoned for many years. We were able to dislodge the warped screen door open and we went in. Only a few minutes inside, I was overcome by a heavy weight of sadness, and all I could do is fall to my knees and weep. I missed something. I could not identify whether I was missing an actual person or event. It was an indefinable sense of grief for something deep within my heart.

After we walked out the front door, I stood on the front porch for a brief moment looking out into the front yard. The view of the dry barren ground, the few struggling trees and feeling the gentle breeze triggered a memory. I remembered one of my repeating dreams. In that dream, I would be standing on a front porch. The porch would be made of wood that was worn and discolored from the weather. The yard would be barren and dry. There were three trees in the yard: Two trees to the left and one to the right of the well-worn pathway leading away from the home. In the dream, I could feel the wind and hear the whistling sound as the wind moves. The dream carried with the visual images the feelings of emptiness and aloneness. Behold, as I stood on the front porch, I felt as though I was actually standing in that scene of my dream. Had it only been a dream? Was it only a coincidence that where I was resembled a memory? Or perhaps was it a real memory that had been stored in the memory banks of my very early infancy? I probably will never know.

Nancy then took me to visit with Seth and Roda and later we went to visit with two of Kate's long-time friends, Abbie and Rachel. Through them, I found out the situation that led to my adoption and something about Kate's character. She had carried an overwhelming sense of shame for an untimely pregnancy. Her society and her community's fundamental religion had been verbally judgmental and cruel. Not only was she shamed, but also, the baby that she was carrying was shamed (it had to be hidden from the world). Her community abandoned her and so did the man she thought loved her. Her closest cousin, who would have been her support, was away at war. I have not been able to find out much about my birth father, Steven, as the information about him has not been forthcoming. This remains a mystery to me, which I pray will one day be revealed.

I came away from the visit with more information than I knew what to do with. Kate was creative, talented, left-handed, witty and strong-willed. She loved to swim and loved to play volleyball. She did not like school and therefore was often absent. Her mother had abandoned her when she was around ten. She and her older sister, Claudia, were sent to live with relatives so that her father, Philip, could continue working. In that home, she became heavily influenced by her Aunt Ada's strict religious belief system. I was told that Kate was taught that only shameful girls got pregnant out of marriage. In her late teens, she married and moved away. She returned with her first child several years later after becoming separated from her husband. She had to work to support herself and her child. When Kate discovered that she was pregnant with me, she faced a crisis. Socially and religiously, she faced shame from her community. Her job, because it was serving the public, would not allow her to work and be pregnant. Her friends, Abbie and Rachel, told me in order to keep her job while pregnant, Kate bound her stomach to give the appearance of being slim. They also told me Kate had hoped this binding would abort the pregnancy. It was not me that she wanted to disappear but the pregnancy. I cannot imagine the agony my birth mother felt as she was torn trying to decide what to do. Abbie and Rachel said they had always wondered, "If I was alright because I had been so squeezed up inside and all that."

In spite of her shame, which led to her attempts to use a home remedy to abort the pregnancy, God had a plan for my life. I now believe it was by His grace that I am alive to share this story. I am grateful Kate failed to abort me. I am grateful to have life. Even with all the struggles my life has given to me, I am alive. Life is a gift from God.

When I imagine how it must have been for Kate to be judged by her relatives and the abusive religious system that was the predominant faith in that particular town, my heart grieves for her. As I have carried my own sense of shame, I could relate to her carrying hers. Was I also carrying Kate's shame and it was not mine to carry? I was seven months old when adopted. What memories and emotions were given to me to carry in that short time? I was told that once I was born, Kate loved me. It was the untimely pregnancy she had not wanted. For emotional and financial reasons, she chose to place me for adoption. I can only imagine the grief she felt. Her friends told me she grieved for me for the rest of her life.

After seven more months of searching, I found my other siblings. When I went to visit them all except for Mark, they had made banners which they had strung out all over their apartment complex, welcoming me to their homes. I was filled with tears and gratitude for all of their love. By getting to know Susanna, Karen, and Pete, I found very special friends. Like Nancy, they are like me in so many ways. Through them, I have come to know Kate in a special way. I have come to know me. I was given the gift of connection to my roots.

It seemed natural for me, at this point, to talk to my mother about my search for my biological roots. At first, she was uncertain as to why I had chosen to search. Once she understood my need to know and my need to find my roots, she went to her office and pulled out of her filing cabinet the social history that the social worker had given to her many years before. She had stored it in a special place to give to me when I was ready. The detailed document filled in all the other details that I had not been able to gather from conversations with Kate's family members. The document did give me information about my birth father, but not where I could find him.

I was both awed by all the people who helped me along the adoption search, by those who accepted me and my mother for her gift of the documents that she had held in secret.

I was blessed because others were willing to share their stories with me. A part of my identity had been missing and, with their help, I was able to put more pieces of my life together.

Chapter 10

An Awakening

*Out of suffering have emerged the strongest souls;
the most massive characters are seared with scars.*

—KHALIL GIBRAN

The discomfort and pain intensified to a critical level beyond my ability to cope with or to tolerate. Running away to stop the pain was a familiar pattern. One afternoon after drinking heavily, I told the children that I would be back; I got in my car, and without any thought other than how badly I was hurting and how badly I needed to get away from the pain, I ran away. I was not consciously choosing to abandon my children but they later told me they felt that I had. I did not stop to hold on to the doorknob this time as I had done several years before while in the therapist's office. Because I had been drinking heavily, I did not get too far down the road before I passed out at the wheel. My car went into an open field, tearing down the owner's fence. The car continued until it hit a tree head-on. My head jerked forward and hit the steering wheel, which broke my glasses. My left eye was bloodshot from the force of impact. I had bruises all over and my chest and my head were sore. The police officer who found me took me to jail and put me in a cell to sleep it off. I was not taken to the hospital to be evaluated for a concussion.

The cruelty of my behavior will live with me for the rest of my life. I had not told my children I was leaving the house and I did not call my husband to let him know where I was. My family had to worry in agony all night regarding my safety. They suffered because of my brokenness and anger. They suffered because I did not seek to resolve the unresolved issues I brought into marriage and motherhood.

In the middle of the night, a person dressed in a uniform came into the cell and held me down while he tore off my underpants and then raped me. I struggled to get away, but I was too weak from the trauma of the accident and too drunk to stop him. My body was already bruised and my head hurt from the concussion. He was stronger than I was. His nasty hand covered my mouth and I could not scream. I would have thought I was dreaming except for the pain of it all. After he finished with me, he left me in agony all alone in the cell. I felt like garbage that had been thrown out and left to rot, full of maggots and any other vile thing that comes to mind. I felt like I had deserved to be treated the way that I had been.

God, where are you? Why have you abandoned me? Why have I been raped again?

I pleaded in prayer but no one answered. Maybe God did not care anymore. Maybe I had stepped across the line of His wanting to be part of my life. I was so empty. The pain of emptiness was unbearable. Self-blame coupled with shame overshadowed my ability to believe God actually still loved me. For that matter, there was no love of myself. How could I file charges against someone that I could not even identify? I had been arrested for drunken driving; who would believe me? Who would believe that the rape had occurred while I was in the jail cell?

The pain of the accident and the rape experience were physically painful to say the least; however, the emotional pain of feeling empty, shamed and utterly and completely abandoned by my friend, God, were even more crippling. Alone and in deep agony, time seemed to stand still. Tears from my heart poured out from the depth of my soul. I felt sick to my stomach. I was uncertain if the nausea was from too much alcohol, the trauma of the accident or the rape. I hurt too badly to throw up, so I tried to lie as still as I could. In the solemn quietness of the night, God did come and He did answer.

Out of nowhere, I saw Christ standing in front of the opening to a cave. The long, white, flowing tunic that He wore was gently blowing in a breeze, His arms outstretched with his nail-scarred palms open. He said to me in a gentle compassionate voice: "My sacrifice saved you not only in and for eternity, but also to live the life that you were created to live right *now* on this earth. I saved you this day to *live*. Satan has played havoc for a time but that is now over." He assured me that the hell I believed I had experienced on earth was nothing compared to the hell of eternity. Was I dreaming or was it real? I did not know which. I did not want to live under the illusion something was true only to find out later that it was false. Some of my illusions had been brought to light in the previous rehab center. I did not want to have an experience of the Divine be an illusion. I do know that the experience and the message made a profound impression on me. (You will learn that later I studied dreams and symbolism. Dreams are real messages from, some say, the unconscious self; others call it the dream maker and still others say it is the Holy Spirit. For me, my experiences were a divine language cocreated from my core being and the Divine to lead me into healing and wholeness.)

Emotionally beaten but grateful that I had not hurt or killed anyone in my drunken driving, I called a friend the next morning and asked her to call my husband. They came together to get me. I needed Barbara, my friend and prayer partner, to be with David when he came to get me, as I feared his wrath. My husband had the right to be angry. I had been so cruel to him. I had made him suffer all night wondering where I might be. I had remained addicted. I had not stopped drinking.

This addiction was powerful and greater than my ability to gain sobriety on my own. My best efforts had failed. The two rehabilitation centers and the continued therapy were slow in helping me to change. I had gained new insights that provided some healing but many more issues were yet to be faced. Change had a cost. I was still so connected to the belief that I needed the approval of my husband that I chose to let go of my healing. He approved of me being sober but to change was to risk his loving the new sober me. I thought that I so desperately needed to be loved by him. I wasn't able to love myself and had projected that responsibility onto him. Abandonment and rejection were rampant in my life, continuing to destroy my relationships. I had no idea what true love was. I had given all of myself to him and there was nothing left of my own identity. Being connected to him was a way of knowing who I was. Separation for me was like a death I had carefully avoided.

David took me to the hospital for a complete medical evaluation, and a probable concussion was decided. I was too embarrassed to admit to having been raped. I did not consciously think any of the following but they may have been part of the desperation I was feeling.

I had shared my first rape experience with him and I remember his turning away from me. Right after David and I were married, I shared with him my experiences about having dyslexia. I felt his response was insensitive to the emotional pain I had experienced. He told me to "get over it." Looking at this in today's light, I can see that because he had just returned from Vietnam, his experiences might have seemed far more traumatic than my life with dyslexia. I did not share the second rape with him because of the history we already shared.

My brain felt like it had a terrible bruise and it hurt. After the ER visit, David took me home. I went straight to the bedroom. I felt so dirty that I could not even sit on the bed, so I sat on the floor with my knees drawn to my chest.

David followed me into the bedroom and said, "After all I have done for you, you have done this to me!"

I asked, "What have you done for me?"

He answered, "*I stayed!* And God knows how hard that has been!" Then he walked out of the room.

Something about the tone in his voice and the words that were said rang like a loud gong in my heart and in my ears. I became dizzy and disoriented. When I refocused, I began to ask myself, "How did I get to this place? Where was the mountain top peace? Where were the changes that had occurred from having met Christ? Where was my God? Raped a second time. How could I have ever let that happen again?" There I was on the floor of my own home, dirty, disgraced, raped and judged as vile by the man who once loved me. I felt his disgust and anger. I was responsible for the drunken behaviors that led me to the floor; as irrational as they were, they were my behaviors. I was not responsible for the rapist's behavior, nor for the attitudes or choices my husband made in response to me.

My soul cried out "I want to live. I will give up whatever it takes to reclaim my dignity, my self-respect and my life. Even if it means I have to divorce or lose custody of my children. I will live life on life's terms. I will be sober." I did not say this out loud. I just kept it in my heart. Somewhere in the middle of confusion, physical pain, and shame, I found hope. It was faint but in comparison to all the other heavy emotions, I was aware that hope existed. I did take a few drinks after that day, but I never again became drunk. When I did start to drink, I relived the night of the wreck and I put the drink down. Putting the drink down was the only way that helped to calm the trauma of that night.

As I convalesced at home recovering from a mild concussion, I had a lot of time for soul-searching what had happened. I had plenty of time to reflect on my behaviors, my attitudes, my choices and what was important to me. I had time to dialogue with God and to make some sense of why I felt abandoned by Him. In one of my prayer times seeking God's presence, I had an answer to my questions about why God allowed me to be raped as a teenager and again as an adult. I believe God said to me the rapes were the result of broken people making hurtful choices. God has given to mankind the gift of free will so that we are not forced to accept His love. The agony of free will is that we can use it to hurt others. When we use our free will in this way, God feels agony for His broken children. He suffers along with His children who suffer. That by no means excuses the rapists' actions. They are wrong and the abusers should be held legally responsible. It just helped me to see that I was part of a broken world and that I have the same power to hurt others. I also have the same responsibility to change my ways as others who, by their actions, words, or even neglect, hurt me. It was only after I could accept that the rapists were themselves in some way broken that I was able to forgive them. My forgiveness of others does not in any way condone what they did.

Three months after the automobile accident, David's employer transferred him to their office in Central Texas. After we were settled in our new home, I began to look for ways that would help me to continue with my recovery program. As part of recovery, I decided to return to college, but I was not sure what degree I wanted to pursue. I was able to narrow my focus to that of a ministry through serving as a psychotherapist or possibly the ordained ministry. I met a woman in our church who was working on her master's degree in social work. I had never known about that degree. I thought that social work was a very narrow field. She convinced me that there were many jobs available in the field. I decided an undergraduate degree in social work was where I would begin. I filled out the application and had a copy of my records sent from high school. Several colleges that I had applied to during my senior year in high school did not accept my application due to my grade point average and I was apprehensive about acceptance this time. To my surprise, I was accepted for the following semester. My children were in junior high and I believed that we could all adjust to my new schedule.

There were a few tasks I needed to accomplish before I started school. First, I wanted to visit Kate's grave. Secondly, I wanted to visit my half-brother, Mark, whom I did not meet at the time I visited with the other siblings. And lastly, I wanted to enter rehab one last time. For my life to be truly set free, I would need to delve into the roots of my alcoholism. I was aware my heart was now open to being truly honest with myself and to taking responsibility for lasting changes.

I went to the cemetery where my Kate was buried. I sat by her grave for hours. I really hoped I would hear some profound message that would fill the hole that had been left there, and this filling would change the course of my life. I wanted to hear all the things I had missed my entire life. I waited. There was only silence. I could hear the wind blowing and smell the freshly cut grass. After a long while, I began to dialogue with her as though she were there. I began to tell her about my life and about me. I talked about the shame that she must have carried because I was illegitimate. I told her how I had carried shame, too. I talked for hours. Sobbing, I told her how much I missed not knowing her.

It suddenly occurred to me I was angry that she was not there to answer my questions; I felt abandoned by her again. The word *"again"* was magnificent. I needed her and she was not there. I had needed her a long time ago and she had not been there.

Healing abandonment issues was bigger than just awareness or cognitive resolution. I actually felt her abandonment of me in the core of my body, heart and mind. It was a familiar feeling. I was angry, resentful, lost, blamed myself, lacking in trust of others and my difficulty bonding with others ran through my emotions and memory. Memories like not trusting my adoptive mother's love for me because I was subconsciously fearful I would be abandoned by her. I began to come to terms with the deep longing for connection I had lived with.

I found that, as the tears flowed, I was able to forgive her for not knowing how much I would ache to know her. Because she did not know, I could forgive her for giving me up for adoption. She gave me the best she could.

Leaving her grave, I felt purged of resentment and anger toward her. At the grave, I also left the shame I believed she had endured and that I had carried for her which was not mine to carry. I had lived under her shame for being pregnant out of wedlock. I was somewhat reconciled to the reality that there would always be unfinished business and questions that were never to be answered. I would never know about my birth father. I would never know about their relationship. I walked away from Kate's grave with a profound love and compassion for her and a connection to the pain she must have gone through for me.

I went to visit Mark in the prison where he was serving time for actions committed while abusing drugs and alcohol. He was on one side of the prison screen and I was on the other. When I came face-to-face with him, I was struck by our physical resemblance. He stated that he, too, had had academic difficulties. He was not able to get the academic assistance I had been given. As I sat and talked with Mark, I was aware how much the combination of my biological roots and my environment had influenced my development. I also understood how this unique combination had come together to form my health, my value system, my faith and had put me into a community that also influenced my formation. My sibling and I were alike in so many ways, yet my environment sent my life in a different direction. Having met my siblings, I saw what my life would have been like if I had been raised by my birthmother and I was so very thankful for being adopted. So many of the issues that I had with my adoptive parents now seemed secondary. I had been given opportunities and adventures that I would not have had if my birthmother had kept me. She was financially lower middle class. The family struggled to make ends meet. Her husband was a janitor and she was a seamstress. The siblings describe her as loving and giving. I do not want to sound like a snob but in reality I was raised in privilege. My parents were able to provide special education in a private school, medical needs and physical therapy, trips across the US and Europe and so much more. I grew up resenting this privilege. I felt singled out and people in the community resented me for it. I grew up with a nanny who was the cook and maid as well as the nanny. Whenever my sister and I would go places with her, I was acutely aware that society did not accept her because she was black. I was confused and heartbroken that she should be treated this way. I loved her and people who hurt her, hurt me, too.

I remember going to church with her one Sunday. My sister and I were joyfully welcomed into the congregation. We danced and played the tambourine as we sang the songs. I felt accepted more than in my own church. However, this day I accepted it as a gift as part of the gift of adoption and life. I accepted that I was to be a good steward of all that I have been given. It was an honor to have both. My birth siblings are special people and I loved them. With this discovery, it was easy for me to choose a degree that blended environment, sociology (the scientific study of social behavior, its origins, development, organization and institutions,) cultural norms and psychology together. Social work as a degree met all those criteria.

My alcohol consumption had almost ceased. I knew I needed one more detoxification center to fortify me. I chose help from a different style of therapy and a different medical treatment program. My brother found information about Dr. Meg Patterson, from England, who developed a revolutionary medical detoxification treatment program named NET: "Neuro-Electric Therapy is a form of electro-medicine. The rapidity of physiological and psychological improvement is impressive. The substantial improvement in depression and anxiety assessments within the short treatment period is unique to this modality."

NET is characterized primarily by: 1. Use of specific combinations of wave-forms, particularly pulse-frequency, as dictated by the drug or combination of drugs under treatment; 2. On-going low-current stimulation over the treatment period; 3. Contraindication of concurrent use of psychopharmacology with the electrostimulation." (Neuro Electric Therapy, Patterson, 1986).

I was unable to go to England for the treatment. However, one of the doctor's nurses came to America to give me the treatment in a secure environment. She used mild stimuli to the brain to change the brain chemistry. Minute electrical currents, self-adjusted to a comfortable level of sensation, are passed across the head via self-adhesive electrodes attached on the mastoid process of the ear (located just behind the ear). Continuous stimulation was administered throughout the entire treatment, twenty-four hours a day. The detoxification program was based primarily on highly specific selections or combinations for the different kinds of abused substances. Other frequencies were integrated into the overall program, specific to alleviating my withdrawal insomnia, cravings, depression, anxiety, fear and agitation. The chemicals in the brain such as serotonin, dopamine and norepinephrine were manipulated to bring my brain back into harmony. The treatment lasted ten days.

As each emotion surfaced, the therapist talked with me and helped me to process them. I did not have to stuff any of these emotions like I had from the previous two centers after discharge from treatment. The treatment was rapid, thorough and safe. A sense of physical well-being, emotional stability and mental clarity were among the most fundamental and potent of the changes. With such a transition came a profound consequence: a belief that my future could change. With change, everything became possible. And with it, I had hope.

By the tenth day, the nurse asked me if I wanted a drink. I was honest and said yes. She went to the medicine cabinet and brought to me my favorite scotch. I was told to drink it. I was rather apprehensive, as I really loved the taste of scotch. I drank it and waited. It tasted really good!

Very shortly, after the scotch had filled my stomach, I began to throw up the scotch and continued to do so for a few minutes. The vomit came from the pit of my stomach. I felt like I was throwing up emotions and garbage from a lifetime. Tears flowed down my face, and I kept repeating, "Thank you. Thank you." An overwhelming sense of gratitude washed over me as the tears continued to flow.

> *An overwhelming sense of gratitude washed over me as the tears continued to flow.*

From that day to the present, the smell of liquor or beer makes my stomach queasy. Drinking again will always be a choice. For the first time in a very long time, I felt sane. I felt I was able to choose to be sober. I felt clear-minded. I was aware that drinking again would take the sanity away. I would not choose to forfeit that ever again. I discovered the root to my addiction was not only anger, as I had thought, but it was also shame, anxiety, grief, broken emotions, unreal expectations about life and taking care of others. The major discovery was the realization that I had given up my own identity to be whatever else others wanted of me in order that they might accept me. I had no identity of my own that I could define. I had lost my ability to say what I believed. I had a vision of myself as physically and mentally retarded. I had seen myself as incapable of succeeding. What I believed about the world around me affected how and what I believed about myself. These beliefs influenced not only how I had related to the self, but also how I related to others. I began to look again at my childhood issues and resentments.

On another level, somewhat deeper than previous explorations, I became aware of my need to be loved and accepted for who I was when I was a child. I was able to look into the lives of my parents as individuals and to see their pain.

As I identified patterns of behavior and beliefs, it became obvious that I had expected my relationship with my husband to heal my past needs stemming from my mother and father relationships. My husband was not and could never be "my father or mother." As wife and mother, I followed in the footsteps of what I had been taught, observed and subconsciously sensed. It was what was in the unconscious that seemed to have the most power on my attitudes and behaviors. My relationship to my parents was mostly dysfunctional. I brought into my marriage the learned behaviors of poor coping skills, secrecy as a manipulative tool, lack of trust and anger. Sobriety required a radical change and it was paramount that I let go of my unrealistic expectations that my parental relationships would be healed by my marriage. What the marriage could do was mirror the emotions and behaviors that needed examination for change. Marriage was not about being a parent to their spouse. It is about being a companion, sharing responsibilities and having respect for each other's beliefs, interests, boundaries, likes and dislikes. Marriage is built on cheering each other up and supporting each other in times of need. Talking openly and honestly all of the time. Listening to one another without a personal agenda. Forgiving when feelings are hurt. It's about caring for and protecting each other. I did not have this kind of role modeling. Parts of it were there, for instance their commitment to the marriage, but I had mostly retained the negative: poor communication and lack of problem solving. I have no idea what my parents' marriage was like behind what I visibly saw. It was time now to let go of the expectation and assumption others would change for me. I made a conscious decision to let go of those resentments and to take responsibility for my own healing.

On Christmas Eve, I left the center with new hope and a healthy sense of well being, never again to return to taking a drink of alcohol. I would not forfeit my sanity for a drink ever again. It has now lasted for over twenty-two years.

God had heard my cry in the wilderness. He had brought me safely through the trial by fire. He had provided a way for me to connect with my biological roots. He opened doors that were closed. He saved my life. He gave me hope. He healed me of alcoholism. He had opened the doors so I could reestablish my relationship with my parents, my husband and my children. He blessed me with a spiritual foundation of rich fertile soil from which all else could grow.

Chapter 11

A New Kind of Education

All discomfort comes from suppressing your true identity.
—BRYANT MCGILL

I began my university studies two weeks after discharge from the rehabilitation treatment facility. Challenged by dyslexia, fear of failure, competitive classmates and the requirement to learn a foreign language, I set my mind and my emotions to the task. All of the tasks required humility, persistence, courage and the willingness to experience stress. Graduate school was part of my overall plan and therefore it was necessary for me to keep a 3.0 or better grade point average in my undergraduate studies. Learning time management in family life was difficult at first. Every step of the way, God's Holy Spirit was there to guide and to heal me. The intimacy with God I knew as a child returned. Through the answer to prayer, a flash of insight, a person who showed up at the right time to be an answer, I found emotional and physical stability. I was doing the work, for God was not doing it for me. I stepped out in faith; then, the answers and intervention followed. I remember one night I was exceptionally weary and my brain was so fatigued that I wasn't thinking clearly. I needed to write a report that was due the next day. I prayed for assistance to finish and I believed that God could and would clear my mind, for scripture writes in I Cor. 2:16 "We have the mind of Christ." I set back to the task at hand and without trouble I finished my report.

Commuting to the university was an eighty-mile round trip. I was eager to begin, so I enrolled in five classes. Studying for those classes took about twenty hours a week. Getting back in the routine of reading and writing was challenging. Our children were in junior high and still needed help with after-school activities and homework. There was the usual house cleaning, laundry, meal planning and prep, being a wife and motherhood. My body would often feel exhausted; yet, the drive to complete a degree was stronger. My time was spread so thin that David and I did not have much time for each other. Most nights our children and I would gather around the dining table and do our homework. I had fun asking them some of my homework questions to hear their responses. The bulk of my studying was done between 11:00 p.m. and 3:00 a.m.

Three-quarters of the way through the first year, I came down with pneumonia. I had pushed myself so hard that my immune system had suffered. I did not regain my health as quickly as I had planned. In fact, I lost my voice for a month. Our children loved that! I was forced to take the next semester a little slower to avoid a relapse. Slowing down a bit gave me time to reorganize time management. I had shifted my obsession from alcohol to school in ways that were subtle. I thought that I had just been focused on my recovery plan. That I was, but reaching wholeness is a balance between all of life's interests and responsibilities.

All of a sudden, I was taking care of myself with more conscious awareness not only of my emotional and cognitive needs, but also of my body's. It seemed so selfish to me as I had always been a caretaker of others. By not spending energy on overcaring for my family, I was able to tolerate stress without falling apart. My family gradually adjusted to their new roles of taking care of themselves. I taught them to do their own laundry and prepare their lunches for school. They were actually glad that I stopped nagging them to do their homework or clean up their rooms. Earning their trust was a little more complicated than getting them to take care of their personal needs. At first, they were suspicious of my intent and behaviors. If I did not get back from school at the exact time they thought I should, they were worried I was running away again. I would call home to let them know I would be late, and it was an adjustment for them to trust that I was telling the truth. Eventually, they trusted that they could believe my words. Recovery from addiction is a family affair. All members have been wounded and all need healing.

My therapist had warned me about possible reactions from family members. The family had learned behavioral and emotional responses to me while I was drinking. These responses had become habits. Change was uncomfortable for everyone. As my responses were changing, my family faced anxieties of their own. Our interaction brought about new responses. Letting go of their need to keep me safe was a hard habit for them to lose. While my family was adjusting to my sobriety, they also were adjusting to the emotional changes both in me and in them. In order for me to remain sober, dramatic changes were necessary. I was claiming my right to be me. I was learning how to put my truth into words. I withdrew from handling as many of the tasks as they were capable of completing on their own. I allowed them to be angry with me and to verbalize it. I was willing to talk through situations without falling apart. It was difficult to hear their version of how I hurt them, coupled with their sense of betrayal. I had wounded them by leaving them the night I had the accident without telling them I was leaving the house. They felt abandoned. I could relate to their feeling of being abandoned and I was full of remorse for their hurt feelings and my behavior. I wanted to avoid or deny. My ears would sometimes deafen the words as my body attempted to shield me from accountability. I stayed in the conversation and accepted responsibility for my actions. Each time we finished our conversations, and

> *I do have remorse for my actions and for the wounding they caused. At times, I remember hurting them and I grieve.*

there were many, a little more healing had been born individually and in our relationship. I experienced a sense of freedom I had not expected. I thought I would feel shame but the truth was healing. I do have remorse for my actions and for the wounding they caused. At times, I remember hurting them and I grieve.

By the sheer nature of remaining sober, I found I was able to cope with increased stress. For example, not having dinner on the table at the right time. That seems simple to a healthy person living life on life's terms. But my need to be perfect used to send me into an "I'm sorry. I'm sorry," in an attempt to avoid the fear of being rejected for my imperfection. I had more energy both for living and for coping.

It was becoming evident to me that the roots of healing for sobriety had been formed in all of my attempts to gain sobriety. God had not abandoned me. Every struggle, including the biological family search, had added to my ability to handle stress and to remain sober.

The very behaviors, emotional responses, and attitudes that drove me into alcoholism were to be the strengths that held me firmly in sobriety.

The very behaviors, emotional responses, and attitudes that drove me into alcoholism were to be the strengths that held me firmly in sobriety. Instead of using those for destructive behaviors, I chose healthy ones. I had been loyal to the bottle. Now I became loyal to sobriety. I had been obsessive and compulsive about drinking.

I would now become focused on school and family. I was persistent in behaviors that led to drinking. I used that energy in moving steadfastly toward new choices that ended in healthy behaviors. I was hypervigilant in avoiding the truth when threatened. I would now be vigilant in pursuing the truth even when afraid.

Finishing two degrees and the hope of being employed became disputed issues. David believed that my employment would be a reflection on his ability to provide for us as a family. He really did not think that my getting a bachelor's degree was necessary and I suspect that is the reason he refused to help lighten my homemaking duties. I felt getting a degree was necessary for my healing journey, necessary for my self-esteem and necessary for my very life. The degree symbolized a major shift from an old negative belief that I was not capable of attaining higher education.

I was beginning to entertain the discrepancy between truth and imagination. It was vital to my self-esteem that I finish my degree. He made several attempts to convince me that finishing school was getting in the way of family life. When none of those attempts had any effect on me, he suggested that we move to another town in the middle of my junior year. This would mean I would have to take longer to finish my degree requirements. I saw it as a sabotage to thwart my successful completion of college. I found that my patience in hoping he would change his mind was wearing then.

One evening he told me that he had begun to seriously search for another job. He had sent in a couple of applications. No! He wasn't going to do this! Adapting to his needs again and putting my needs aside was not an option for me. Finishing school would be accomplished. I became angry and resented him. After a few seconds of looking for a way to cope, I shouted: "I will not go with you until I finish my degree. In fact, I will go on for my master's and then I will follow you. The children will stay here with me." I hadn't planned to be so bold but it actually felt good.

My changes became threats to our marriage. I was becoming assertive and self-motivated. I was changing from the person who was solely motivated by what others wanted me to be. There was a fine line in securing my path and in accommodating those in my family. The fine line also included the difference between selfishness and self-preservation. I was not sure at that point I was able to complete all my studies and motherly duties effectively, but I was doing my best to learn new skills.

Staying up very late hours to study was necessary. It was the only time I had when everything was quiet and no one needed me to do something. A strange thing happened. When we previously relocated to West Texas, David began to drink alcohol socially. He had not become addicted to it as I had. His favorite was bourbon and mine was scotch. After I started school, David switched his choice of liquor to scotch. I think this response was probably subconscious, but nonetheless, the statement that it made was the same. Just before his going to bed, he would pour himself a tall glass of scotch and water. He would come by the table where I was studying, kiss me goodnight and leave the glass of scotch at the end of the table. The first night he did that, I thought it was a mistake.

However, when it became routine, I would hear the words of my therapist ring out: "Expect sabotage."

Each morning I would mention to him that he had left his drink on the table and he could pour it out. In spite of David's reasons for leaving the glass there, I grew to see that glass as my victory over my desire to drink. I suspect that his identity included his need to take care of me. It was disorienting for him not to need to worry or spend time or effort in protecting our children or me from my drinking behavior. His role as protector was who he was. He needed help in adjusting to not needing to care for me but his pride prohibited him from getting that help. He was not prepared for the changes I was making in myself. Our relationship was changing and he could not control it. He wanted that old Jeanne back: the one who had, more often than not, forfeited her needs or wants for whatever someone else wanted, the woman who gave of herself until there was nothing left to give. The *always* giving woman was the person he loved. He treasured my ability to mold my love and life to meet his needs and the world around us. I had given so much that an empty vessel had developed. There is a vital difference between the illness of codependency and that of true Christian compassion. I had been a sick codependent.

I saw serving others as Christian service consciously and as a deliberate decision. Subconsciously, I was also meeting my psychological need to be approved of and be accepted. My own identity was steeped in codependency. As a child, my position in the family was "the fixer." I naturally grew to adulthood living in the same role caught between the fixer and my deep longing to serve with Christian compassion. Christian compassion is about loving others. That does not mean always giving all or doing everything for them. Sometimes, saying "no" to helping or intervening is a healthy response. A fixer/codependent is one whose motive is self-serving. It becomes my need to make my pain go away by stopping or alleviating yours. Old habits are hard to break. It begins with awareness. Now I could see the traps I had built and I had more tools to dissemble to them.

Somewhere along the way, I lost the person who was created in the image of God's son. Discovering this person again was a struggle and required hard work. My life depended on finding her again. I believe that David did not evaluate our relationship as I did. Leaving his glass of scotch there may have meant, in a kind of twisted way, that he wanted me to be as close to him again as when we first married. My heart, also, yearned to be close to him again. Neither one of us knew how to say it or work through our differences. We had been in love and we were so happy when we first married. I believed both of us were grieving the loss of our relationship and what it could have been had circumstances been different.

David slipped into a depression of his own. I was growing, changing, becoming self-confident and verbal. He withdrew inwardly, not seeking any emotional help from anyone. It was no longer healthy for either of us for me to be his caretaker and provide his emotional work for him. I could not be both in counseling for my issues and counselor to him. Any time one partner changes, it affects the way the other responds. Change requires a response. Change is scary. I ran out of patience with his inability to change. Had I been in a different place, and had I been able to wait until he had had sufficient time to change, maybe the marriage would have survived this crisis. I just could not do the work for both of us. No one can. It's the codependent's fallacy. My life was taking on a completely different shape from what it had been in the past. I admit I was apprehensive about what the future would look like. I was not even sure of who I would become. Stepping into the unknown takes courage and a belief that the risks are worth it.

By this time, I had already worked on my issues in therapy for close to five years. I had neither the energy nor the desire to work any longer on our marriage. We were at a crisis point and I could not save both of us. We grew farther and farther apart. He had stayed with me during my drinking days and now I was not willing to stay with him. He said that to me so many times. I felt like I had to choose between abandoning him or me. I felt so guilty for wanting to leave him. I tried to fill my days with classes, homework and helping the children in an attempt to postpone those feelings. I hoped that time would heal our marital stresses.

Healing came in so many ways during my undergraduate time. The first semester back in college, I actually made the dean's list. I was satisfied that I could achieve the scholarly excellence. After having pneumonia, I decided I would be a solid "B" student, relax, enjoy the school experience and to have fun with my family. I did not need to make the dean's list ever again.

The semester following the dean's list award, I made a thirty on my first test in economics. I never connected with the subject matter. It did not make sense to me. I learned much more easily when things made sense to the way my brain works. Oh, I was so embarrassed! Oh well. I showed steady progress through the course, and although I did not make the actual grade, the professor gave me a C because of the effort I had made.

There were many times when I would make the top of a grade bracket and the professor would bump the grade to the next letter. They all knew how hard I was trying. I am thankful for all those who saw my effort and helped me along the way.

Learning Spanish was a challenge. I remember about a month into Spanish class, the teacher asked her students to read out loud in Spanish the answers to our homework from the night before. I had a panic attack! My memory zoomed backward to the first grade when I was just beginning to read sentences and having to pronounce unfamiliar words. To avoid having the class members observe my emotional meltdown, I ran to the ladies' room and hid out in one of the stalls shaking and rocking back and forward. In a prayer, I asked God to allow His Holy Spirit to walk me through this memory so that I could move forward.

There is no way to define the humiliation of shame to someone who has never felt its weight. My heart was in agony as I felt shame. My body began to hurt and shake. I felt weak and almost faint. After what seemed an eternity, I found myself grieving for the little girl who was shamed at such a young and innocent age. This little girl was a part of myself that I had been afraid to connect with. Now I was and an overwhelming sense of compassion for her flowed through my tears. I sat for a few minutes and then went back to class. When it was my turn to read, I was still afraid of the sound of my voice but I was able to read. The Spanish teacher never did make fun of the pronunciation nor did my fellow students. I was learning I could actually say and make a mistake separate from believing I *was* the mistake.

In all classes, we were required to give verbal presentations. Performance anxiety and I were very old friends. Fearfully, I would stand before my classmates, clutching my report, with sweat rolling down my face. My voice would quiver as I attempted to read aloud. To my surprise, no one made fun of me, and I grew more confident.

I had been given the gift of motivation and stamina. Persistence followed very closely. I felt the presence of God's Holy Spirit every day in all situations and through each decision. The Spirit was my counselor, guide, comforter and protector. He even found me parking spaces and paid my tuition. That may seem strange, but when I was running late and couldn't find a parking space, one would appear after a prayer of request. I was also able to save enough money to pay my tuition. I started with my undergraduate work and attended class through the summers and on through the master's program. I finished in three years, even with having to miss classes due to a bad case of pneumonia and surgery (another bout of endometriosis produced a small tumor that needed to be removed). I look back on this period of time and I am amazed I was able to finish. Each day of sobriety brought about more confidence in my desire to continue in the discovery of what I was capable of accomplishing.

David and I continued to experience stress in our marriage. I sensed that we had moved beyond our ability to save it. Nineteen years previously, I had stood at the altar of my church and promised to remain married to David no matter what challenges our marriage held. My parents counseled me to stay with David. It was their belief that a commitment to marriage was far stronger than any personal need I may have. I was failing at that commitment. Shame raised its head again. I did not want to remain married, and at the same time, I did not want to go against my word. Some of my friends said that God's Word said divorce was not an option and I had to stay married. I sought my minister's counsel and he was not so dogmatic. He was able to assure me that God sees the heart and would forgive me in whatever decision I made. It was not an easy decision. The time of indecision was wrought with fear, uncertainty, blame and responsibility. I had to weigh the consequences and know there would be persons who would not agree with my reasons or choices. I talked with my mother whose belief in marriage was that we were to stay together no matter what. She counseled that marriages have stages and in the end everything works out. Looking back on her marriage, I was not so sure about that. But it was her counsel and I thanked her for it. I sought counseling from a therapist and took away from that session the reaffirmation that I had the right to my needs. Staying or leaving the marriage was secondary to the quality of the marriage. Both partners must make changes in order for the marriage to be healthy. She asked me if I wanted to live in an unhealthy environment.

Torn between these pulls, I spent much time in soul-searching. I fasted and prayed for answers. I prayed for a miracle that would instantly heal both of us. I wanted to honor my promise to God and my commitment to David, Andrew and Ruth. I would be responsible for the hurt to them caused by divorce. If I stayed, I would spare them that pain. I ran head-on into the realization that remaining married was a death sentence to my soul and I wanted to live. The disease of chaos and discord within the marriage was like a malignant tumor. What was I going to do?

> *The decision to divorce was a lonely one I had to make all by myself.*

The decision to divorce was a lonely one I had to make all by myself. In prayer, I felt the forgiveness for my mistakes and the grace to rebuild my life. Honoring my God and honoring myself required that I live in my truth. With an agony of heart, I told David I wanted a divorce and I filed the legal documents.

After talking with his mother, David insisted I had to move out of the home. I had no income and no job. I was still a full-time student. Ruth, now a freshman in high school, and I left with the clothes on our backs to begin again. My parents cosigned with me on an apartment lease, and I later was able to get some furniture and our clothes. Ruth and I spent the first night in our new apartment on the floor crying ourselves to sleep. By the grace of

God, I found a part-time job that gave us enough money for food for our table.

Andrew and Ruth were caught in the pain of divorce. Both children wanted to be with their dad and with me. They wanted us to "just work things out." These were adult problems and were not easily solved. All of us hurt.

When I moved out of our home, Andrew chose to stay with his father. He felt responsible for taking care of his dad. He sensed depression increasing and his dad's drinking behavior pick up. Andrew said he was afraid for his dad. Because both children were at the legal age that they could decide, the courts allowed their decision. Both David and I shared the loss of a child in our home. Andrew and Ruth lost the benefit of being able to share their everyday lives with each other. Divorce is hurtful, and every one for several generations suffers in some way.

The year waiting for the divorce to become final had many ups and downs. I was on an adventure to discover who I was and what I liked and disliked. What was important to me? What were my true feelings? I had given so much of myself away that I did not know who Jeanne was.

Our apartment did not have any fans. I decided to install one myself. I carefully followed the instructions and behold the fan worked! That was fun. The downside was I was grieving the loss of my marriage. I think I was grieving more for what it could have been rather than what it had become. We did not have any money to spare. The tight budget did not allow new clothes. There were times my daughter went to school wearing ragged jeans. Ragged and torn is popular now, but then it was not. We had an old car and she wanted me to drop her off a block away from school so the other students wouldn't see the car.

Andrew and Ruth's father had always been emotionally distant. He was not comfortable either talking about or owning his emotions, other than anger. They got their feelings hurt many times. I remember one day they were both at my apartment and their dad said something that caused Ruth to burst into tears and Andrew to act out in anger. I was enraged! The thought raced through my mind that if I had had a gun and if David had walked through the door at that precise moment, I probably would have shot him. This thought scared me. Where did this violent thought come from? I felt like a mother lioness protecting my young from danger. I chose to hold my emotions in and help Andrew and Ruth work through their pain. Later I called a friend and she said, "You have now let go of your marriage and you can now go on with your life. You are clearly seeing what the relationship was doing to you, to Andrew and to Ruth."

I know that we all have a beast that lives within. It has power over us to raise its destructive head until we are aware of its reality. No devil made me think that I should shoot David. Those thoughts came from within me and they needed to be voiced. But in a safe environment, not exploding on the spot. Family violence is steeped with unresolved beasts that break forth through our ability to keep it suppressed. I had someone to talk to and this helped face the root. Had I not had someone to talk to, I would have needed to seek a therapist. The rage I had just experienced never manifested itself in me again.

I swore I would not date again. I was so completely against relationships and I was happy discovering that I could do things for myself. I discovered that I really had been an efficient homemaker prior to my drinking. I liked being a single person. It was like a calm after a hurricane. I was picking up the pieces and rebuilding my life. Eventually I met someone I wanted to get to know. The children could accept their dad dating but not their mom. Andrew was so angry that he refused to come for overnight visits with us in my apartment.

It is a natural response for children to resent their mom being with another man. My son would ask, "Why can't you and Daddy get back together?" Dating reminded them that their parents were not going to get back together. Dating can be processed as a betrayal of the sanctity of the family. It is also difficult for children to share their mother with a stranger. When I had a date, I had to leave my daughter in the apartment alone. Even though she was a teenager, it was not a good situation. She was apprehensive while I was away and would sit up waiting for me to come home. To reduce the opposition and anxiety, I ceased dating for a while. I did not resent either child. I had caused them enough pain already and my dating could wait.

I did not need to be in a relationship to feel whole. It was actually the opposite. I was learning to be whole so that I could enjoy a relationship as an equal to a mate, not subservient, as I had been.

Waiting gave me time to learn about rebound relationships and how to avoid them. It gave me time to understand why I had chosen David and about the relationship dynamics between us. It is common to marry someone who is a stand-in for a dysfunctional parent. Subconsciously, it is believed that we can resolve the issues we had with a parent in the marital relationship. This is an illusion, for healing comes only when the issues are squarely faced. We own the problem. And we own the responsibility to find the method and the support for change.

It was university policy for all students to take the same exit exam, which really had nothing to do with the student's degree. All students were tested on the same subjects. I have always struggled to take a multiple-choice exam. I would find two of the choices too close to distinguish between. It just so happened that the exit exam was a multiple-choice format. I flunked this exam! Now what? I had a 3.4 GPA, and I would not be allowed to graduate because of some exam that had nothing to do with my degree. School policy required that only those who passed the exit exam would be awarded a diploma. For those who did not pass the multiple-choice exam, there was a written form. As the room full of students gathered to be tested again, I felt a heavy anxiety. This was my last chance. I did pass this one! On graduation day (1987), I was the last student to walk across the stage. My children and parents were shouting for me as I took that miraculous walk. I wept with pure joy that I had been awarded a college degree. What a milestone for a child with a learning disability.

I cried all the way through taking my Graduate Record Examination (GRE). The tears kept me from seeing the questions, so I just marked the little squares as best as I could. I do not believe that I passed. I had applied both to Presbyterian Theological Seminary for a Master of Divinity and to Our Lady of the Lake University for a Master of Social Work. By God's grace, I was accepted into both graduate programs. I was undecided about which was the best path for me. While in undergraduate school, I began to feel called to the ordained ministry. I had weathered the Presbyterian Church's discernment process with its vigorous verbal examinations.

I remember one particular session in which the interviewer said: "You obviously need psychotherapy to solve your unresolved psychological issues stemming from dyslexia." He assured me that the priesthood was an inappropriate place for that. Then he said, "The priesthood is not the place to run from the problems that you are having in your marriage. I suggest you stay home and tend to your husband."

I was offended. He knew my dyslexic history but not my marital history. I responded: "As this is the discernment process I understand your questioning my motives and my vulnerabilities. I am confident of my calling by God. Please give me examples from our conversations together how you have come to your conclusions." All the while I was steaming inside. It was difficult for me to be objective. My feelings were hurt and I wanted to run out of the room, quitting any more interviews with him. I stayed, held my dignity and passed his grueling scrutiny. The Seminary was in another town. David refused to move with me. Our marriage was falling apart and I was not willing to move out of town by myself, commuting back on weekends. After making the decision to divorce David, I felt unworthy to enter the ordained ministry. By default, I chose social work. I came to realize that the ordained ministry is not the only path to serving God. I was actually more suited to be down in the trenches with my clients rather than in the pulpit. I have never regretted my decision.

After a few weeks' break between degrees, I was back in class for more learning. Graduate school was highly competitive. I was told that graduate classes would be more of the same subjects as in undergraduate, but I was not prepared for the increase in the level of academic difficulty.

I found a part-time job to pay the bills, which allowed me to be able to continue with my master's degree program. Adding to the difficulty of the part-time job and the pressure of school was the fact that I was in limbo between the filing for divorce and the final decree. Andrew and Ruth were hurting and I felt responsible for their pain.

I slipped into a mild form of depression. I would sleep. Ruth would wake me and tell me to get up. I would get up, go into the living area, and there, I would sit on the couch staring out the window. This pattern repeated itself for days. Ruth called one of my fellow classmates and asked her to come over to talk with me. The friend helped me to take the feelings and the situation and embrace them from a therapist's point of view. I would need to remember what I was feeling so I would be able to relate to my clients in a special way. By the grace of God, I was brought out of depression and back to the business of school. I did cry often and so did Ruth.

Keeping in touch with Andrew had its own unique set of circumstances. Our divorce was finalized in 1987. David and I remained emotionally at war with one another. Since Andrew was living with David, I would call the house to talk to him. If David answered, he would vent his frustrations out on me. I was not emotionally in a place where I wanted to subject myself to such stress. I had to choose carefully the times when I would call his house. Andrew later said that he felt neglected for my not calling enough. He turned to the mothers of his friends for advice.

Even though I understood, my heart still broke. Parenting a child when the other spouse has custody is painful, especially when it is the mother-child relationship. I had bonded with my children because it is the nature of motherhood but also because I knew what it was like not to have that. The relationship with my son was strained but the love remained strong.

I was awarded a master of social work in 1988, a testimony to another miracle. I studied for and sat for the first required social work licensing exam. The first and the second time that I took the exam, I flunked it. I made a sixty-nine, then a sixty-two. A passing grade was a seventy. I was freaking out. The thought of having come this far and not being able to get a license was exceptionally stressful. My employer had said I would no longer be employed if I did not pass. I was under great pressure. I kept saying the mantra: "I am capable of passing this exam and therefore I will."

The test was a multiple-choice exam. It was difficult for me to choose the correct answer. I answered the questions the way I thought they should be answered but the political slant was different from mine. Therefore, I flunked. I had been determined not to ask for special academic help because of my dyslexia. But this time, I petitioned the certification board and asked if there was assistance for students who were dyslexic. It turns out I was able to go to the testing facility and practice test taking using several of the old tests. I read the questions and the correct answers until my eyes were tired. I had one day to accomplish my task. Fearfully, I repeated the exam. I did pass! I passed with a high grade and became a Licensed Master Social Worker (LMSW).

My goal was to become a licensed psychotherapist and, therefore, one more level of certification must be completed. The licensing board required a five-year internship be completed prior to sitting for the exam. I used these years to gain as much experience in the most varied areas as possible. I had no idea what I would consider to be my area of expertise.

I consider myself a shy but friendly person. I have a difficult time meeting new people or interviewing. I have to force myself to be in a group setting. I have a mild to moderate case of social and performance anxiety which causes me to avoid public speaking engagements whenever possible. My face will flush, and I get queasy in my stomach when called upon to talk about something in front of people, probably part of the residue left from being humiliated in elementary school. I am able to talk one-on-one very well. However, on one specific rare occasion, I took a chance. I went to a National Association of Social Workers annual conference, not knowing anyone. The people at my lunch table were friendly and I quickly forgot my nervousness. The following business day, I received a call from the Personnel Director in a psychiatric hospital in east Texas offering me a job. He had been one of the persons at my conference table. I felt stronger emotionally and thought I would be able to handle any stress that a new town or a new job presented. I had walked through a divorce, earned two degrees, worked successfully in a variety of jobs helping others to sort through family issues and to face health situations, job-related questions, adoption, chronic or terminal illnesses, disability, faith crises, rape or other violent actions, grief and losses. The timing was right for me to leave central Texas; I accepted the position. It was 1992 when I set out from central Texas. It was a strange feeling as I saw San Antonio in the rearview mirror. Flashbacks of the agony and despair coupled with the monumental growth life had showered upon me whizzed through my mind. I had to chuckle when I remembered that Saint Anthony is the saint to whom we pray to help us find things. And certainly, although I had never prayed to him, the thing I found was myself.

Moving gave me an opportunity to live closer to my parents' home. After the discharge from the second rehab center, my relationship with my parents had begun to develop in a way that was healing for all of us. I felt Mother and I had begun to talk more openly. She was both mother and friend. I was able to accept both parents for who they were and not what I had wanted or needed them to be. There was a sense of freedom when I allowed my parents to be who they were, knowing they were the same people they had always been. Accepting their weaknesses and forgiving them for their inability to meet all my needs was freedom from disappointment and their rejection. I had spent so many years yearning to feel connected with them, and now it was a reality.

Chapter 12

EVERYTHING IS CONNECTED

I believe that life is chaos, a jumble of accidents, ambitions, misconceptions, bold intentions, lazy happenstances and unintended consequences, yet I believe that. There are connections that illuminate our world, revealing its mystery and wonder.

—DAVID MORANIS

Moving to this new town gave me an opportunity to step out of my comfort zone. Talking to strangers had never been easy for me. And there I was; everyone was a stranger. I had to push myself every time I engaged in conversation with an unknown person. Eventually meeting people became a game for me to see how many new individuals I could meet that day. The numbers of strangers shrank and soon I was at home.

I had never worked in a psychiatric hospital before. Working with patients to help them reestablish coping and life skills so that they could return to society had both challenges and blessings. I remember a special woman named Annie. She had decided that she no longer needed her meds, so she stopped them. Her life became a jumble of confusion and bazaar behaviors. It took several weeks to stabilize her medicines before we were able to have a rational therapy session. During our sessions, she shared a nightmarish dream with me. She asked me to help her with it, for the details of the dream frightened her. Halfway into telling her dream, she started screaming and waving her fists at me.

She stood up and lunged toward me, but stopped short of touching me. It happened so fast that I only had time to shove my chair back a few inches. I said to her: "Wow, you are really angry. What's going on?" She looked confused but sat down. After a few seconds, she said: "You are listening! You are not shutting me up." I asked: "How is it that you are surprised?" She said: "No one has ever allowed me to speak about it. Everyone said I was making it up and to shut up." Her answer was so similar to other stories I have heard. A trusted uncle had repeatedly raped her. To avoid the reality of it, she disconnected from the events. While she did have a chemical imbalance that required a physician monitor her medication, her symptoms were exacerbated by all the secrets she hid. The details came rolling out and the tears and anger flowed. She left my office that day with a sense of being validated. All of us need to feel validated. Her example was a visual expression of that need. While discovering the truth is critical, for her being validated was more important than anything else. Her understanding of the truth was her reality. She grew up with family members accusing her of lying and just trying to get her uncle in trouble as well as trying to divide the family. She was discharged only to return six months later, another episode of stopping her meds.

Many families and society at large are not equipped to understand how to relate in a healthy way to their loved one who suffers from mental illness. The CDC reports that about 25 percent of US adults have a mental illness. Educating oneself about mental illness is a loving gift to give your loved one.

Only one situation influenced my choice to leave the psychiatric hospital after a year. One day on the ward, five men circled me, all clamoring for my attention. Each one believed that his need for attention was the most important of all. I was unable to meet their needs all at the same time. As they began to become agitated, the circle around me tightened. As their agitation elevated and the circle became tighter around me, I became intensely afraid they might attack me. I had worked on the unit long enough to know such an encounter was possible and the staff members, who had been the focus of the patients' anger, were hurt significantly. Their agitation escalated to a yelling match. I was struggling to contain my terror.

Another staff member saw my distress and came to my rescue by shouting at them from across the room: "Hey, you men, she can't help you, I can, so come over here!" The men were startled and turned to see who had shouted at them. This left a hole in the circle for me to escape. I quickly moved out of the circle into my comfort zone. Eventually the men did calm down and everything was all right. I was so unnerved, however, that I spent the evening on my couch shaking from the trauma. This encounter triggered a memory of my dad screaming at me. I remembered not knowing what would happen then and I did not know what would have happened there at the hospital that day. The feeling of not being able to defend myself or even know how to respond to threatening situations was paralyzing. I was emotionally responding as though I was a child. My "would have been" adult response vanished under the trauma of the situation. If I did not face my inadequacies and learn how to respond in trauma, I would, in the future, place others and myself in danger. I thanked God for showing me again how scared I would get when Dad would yell at me or threaten to kill my siblings and me. I had purposely forgotten that part of my life in order to survive. I wanted to remember only the good part of my dad. We did have so many good memories that I wanted them to be the focus of my memory. The sheer reliving of the memory triggered by my work experience was healing. I was able to validate the feelings of the scared little child who lived within me. The child didn't have the coping skills to process the effects of trauma, but the adult did. I was responsible for my healing and so I took responsibility.

> *The sheer reliving of the memory triggered by my work experience was healing.*

I decided it was best for the patients and for me that I seek employment elsewhere. I chose a position at a physical rehabilitation hospital. Medical stabilization had been accomplished and now it was about the work of living with their specific physical needs. Fearing repeat injuries, societal acceptance and limited physical accomplishment, the gifts that the patients gave me were visual witness to their persistent courage in times of pain. Grief is a process, not an event. In the process of assisting patients, I found so many of the issues I had faced as a young preteen.

After the required three years of a supervised internship post-graduation, I was eligible to sit for the next exam. The exam was routinely given in several regions at designated university sites. Due to an overflow of applicants for the test date I had requested, the upper level exam was scheduled at an alternative site. I was surprised to discover that the alternative site was the high school I had attended! What a coincidence!

Going to Hockaday School that day to take the exam brought back so many memories of all the academic struggles that I had overcome. With a deep sense of pride, I took and passed the exam. When it was over, I sat on the curb waiting for my ride with tears of joy streaming down my face. I felt an awesome sense of gratitude for having been a student at Hockaday. The Hockaday teachers had believed I was able to learn with higher standards and higher levels of intuition. They had pushed me to reach my limit with support, tutoring in other subjects when needed, a reading teacher, and scholastic incentives. I was given the opportunity to learn, to develop and to rebuild a healthier self-esteem. They gave me an academic foundation on which to build for the rest of my life. My parents had given to me the gift of being able to attend classes there. While they were not able to build academic excellence or a healthy self-esteem relating to scholastic performance, they made the necessary sacrifices that enabled me to attend Hockaday. Because of the scholastic foundation I had been given there, I was able to earn a master's level degree and to qualify for a professional license.

In my new town, I found a church home. I began to attend a Bible study for singles and because of the intensity of the topic we were studying, we made very deep friendships quickly. I had decided never to marry again out of fear of making another mistake. The intensity of pain that had occurred as the result of my decision to divorce was something I never wanted to put others through or experience again myself.

At first I was able to keep my distance, mainly out of fear of talking. The study group had been together about a year when, to my surprise, I found I was able to engage in conversation with others with less fear. Meeting new people is always a challenge for me. I tend to remain reserved not because I am a snob, but rather because I don't know what to say; the fear of talking shuts my voice down. As I felt more comfortable sharing myself, I was able to relax and truly listen to others.

There was one particular man whose life story was similar to mine. I was more interested in hearing his story and learning how he coped than in flirting with him. Since I was comfortable being single, getting to know him was neither a threat nor a motive to seek a date. The evolution of our relationship seemed natural and unplanned. We were strangers, then acquaintances rapidly becoming friends. The Bible study was a means for talking about our losses, hopes and dreams. It was a place to share where we were in our life's journey and what choices we made that brought us to that point. Dolph and I continued our conversations beyond the group. Our twosome conversations continued to delve deeper and deeper into each other's lives. I began to respect and honor him. Somewhere along the way, I realized I was in love with him.

Love itself brought a combination of polarizing emotions. First, joy, then fear raised its ugly head. I began to question my ability to choose and my ability to make a decision. I feared being wrong again. I had lost my ability to trust my intuition when it came to love. Memories of the trauma of the divorce came echoing back. I feared loss of control. I had been single now for seven years and I was not sure I wanted to give up that independence. My time was my own. My finances were my own. I was concerned I would return to my old habit of forfeiting my right to make my own decisions. I was afraid I would again return to standing in my husband's shadow. I feared the loss of healthy boundaries. I questioned my emotional healing and whether or not I would feel emotionally safe in a new relationship. I feared the rage that went with my previous breakup.

As Dolph and I began to date, I resisted allowing my heart to fall in love with him. I feared if I began to trust him, in a few years or so it would end in disillusionment. He understood my history of alcohol abuse. Even though he drank beer, I did not think that it would bother me.

One night when we had been out on a date, he had a few beers. He usually kissed me good night on the cheek. This night when he brought me home, he kissed me on the lips. I tasted the beer from his mouth; I smelled it, and I remembered! I remembered the entire nightmare. The entire nightmare! I could not put myself in the position that reminded me of that horrible period of time in my life and in the lives of my children. Tears rolled down my face as I sank to the floor with the burden of heavy sadness. I would have to give him up if he wanted to keep drinking. I had grown fonder of Dolph than I realized and the thought of losing him was painful.

With intense emotions, I said to him: "I did not think that your drinking would bother me. However, it does. I cannot continue to date you if you continue to drink."

Dolph said: "I will give it up. You mean more to me than the beer."

I said: "This means never again. Not even when you are out with the men. You would come home, and I would still smell it."

He said that he would never again drink beer or anything that had liquor in it. I did not trust myself in committing to a relationship again. I was afraid I would make another mistake. I did not trust that a partner would honor my needs. I was apprehensive that in a new relationship there would be discord when we were on different paths. I needed someone who, while they may not agree with all my decisions, would be open to discussions. It was important to have him listen, really listen, to me. I was so moved by his response and his commitment to me that I allowed myself to fall in love with him without any more reservations.

Dolph and I were both committed to honesty and openness when talking about our feelings. We dated long enough to have arguments, misunderstandings or hurt feelings and find resolution. It was important for each of us to experience how we problem-solve amid a disagreement. Could we accept the shortcomings of each other when the result of the shortcoming wounded the other? Would either of us hold grudges? Were we capable of forgiveness or would we harbor resentments? Were we good listeners or might there be an undercurrent of different thoughts that keep the other only half-listening? Were both of us able to at times give up what we wanted to support the other? Were we able to be vulnerable in the middle of deep emotional crises? We experienced the death of both his brother and my longtime school friend Beth and we grieved together.

When we were sure that we were comfortable in our ability to communicate our thoughts and needs, he asked me to marry him. We went to our minister to assist us in preparing for marriage. He asked us to take the Myers–Briggs Type Indicator (MBTI) assessment, a psychometric questionnaire designed to measure psychological preferences in how people perceive the world. The purpose of the test for us in the premarital counseling was to help us further our understanding of each other and of ourselves. The results showed that we are different in two distinct areas. I like to solve a problem and am goal oriented; I drive to finish my goal even at the expense of enjoying the journey. Dolph would rather experience the journey on the way to a goal. I tend to pay a great deal of attention to reality, particularly to what I can learn from my own senses; I tend to focus on facts and details and enjoy getting hands-on experience. Dolph prefers to pay more attention to things like patterns and impressions; he enjoys thinking about possibilities, imagining the future and abstract theories. Our minister counseled that this was an area where each of us needed to be patient with the other. This counsel has been exceptionally helpful over our years of marriage. While neither of us can understand how or why we think this way, we can accept that it is part of our personality. Over the years, we have strived to become closer to the opposite perspective, so that we may one day reach a middle ground. After counseling with the minister was completed, we set a wedding date.

In November of 1995, Dolph and I stood at the altar of our Episcopal church and pledged before friends, family and God to love and honor one another forever. Dolph has blessed me beyond my wildest dreams. With him, I feel emotionally safe, an experience I have rarely had. He is sweet and tender. He honors me. He is honest and provides wise counsel when asked. We can disagree and still honor the other's position. He supports and encourages me. We share mutual enjoyments, such as our love of nature. It is a special blessing for me to have a partner who wants to share the journey in faith with me. I can freely give back to him because I love him. Our relationship gives me a sanctuary in which to grow and to develop. I am grateful that he is the companion of my soul.

Marriage the second time around had some different qualities for both of us. We had a handbook about what had been both positive and negative experiences. We were more mature. We had more experiences in relationship building. Life experiences in themselves created a different perspective of self, which enhanced our marital relationship. We had developed communication skills that assisted us in expressing our wants and needs. We had a better understanding of who we were as individuals and were not dependent upon the other to make that definition. We chose to allow each other to grow in the direction that life was calling us. Both of us were willing to compromise and to make sacrifices when needed. We did not have specific expectations of a husband or wife role. It was important for both Dolph and me to develop the ability to be comfortable in sharing responsibilities. We were able to blend, to be individuals or to seek the same path. We had more in common. We were on the same journey of life. Our sense of what was important changed over time, which led to choosing a different mate.

I am grateful that he is the companion of my soul.

After marriage, one of the groups that we joined as a way of journeying along the same path was one whose purpose was to explore various faith traditions both cultural and spiritual. A group of people from many different faiths met once a week to explore the dimensions and expressions of spirituality. We briefly discussed the traditions of spiritual practices in many different traditions: Native American, Sufi, Buddhism, Eastern Orthodox, Early Christian Fathers, Catholic Mystics and Judaism. We also briefly touched on the Kabbalah, Hinduism, Taoism and Polytheism religions, such as Egyptian and Babylonian. An interesting side note was the study of The Epic of Gilgamesh, perhaps the oldest written story on Earth. It comes to us from Ancient Samaria and was originally written on twelve clay tablets in cuneiform script. It recounts the adventures of the historical King of Uruk (somewhere between 2750 and 2500 BCE). The first surviving version of this epic, known as the "Old Babylonian" version, dates to the eighteenth century BCE. Strangely, there are many references to various themes, plot elements and characters in the *Epic of Gilgamesh* that have counterparts in the Hebrew Bible, notably the accounts of the Garden of Eden, the advice from Ecclesiastes and the Genesis flood narrative. The study of this book brought up the study of dreams (outside that of the Bible) and the hero's journey. A hero is a man who leaves the comfort of his home and goes out on an adventure. He encounters struggles and hardships. These experiences transform him before he returns home to lead others along the Hero's path. Gilgamesh has a dream about his future and his downfall. He does not listen and pays the price of misery. This study led naturally into the study of dreams in the Bible and to the philosophy of Dr. Carl Jung. According to Jung, dreams are a way of communicating and acquainting our self with the unconscious. Dreams are not attempts to conceal our true feelings from the waking mind, but rather are a window to our unconscious. They serve to guide the waking self to achieve wholeness and they offer a solution to a problem we are facing in our waking life. Bible dreams reveal a direct communication from the Divine. A kind of spirituality in itself. The Christian mystics like Teresa of Avila were well acquainted with dreams and visions from the Divine.

To further our understanding of various traditions, we went on multiple retreats to experiential learning adventures. The more I learned about other traditions, the more I could see God the creator in all things. I learned to appreciate and expand my own spiritual practice. Reverend Gene Baker, a wise Episcopal minister, spiritual director and licensed therapist with a Jungian orientation, led the group. He led retreats and experiential learning pilgrimages. We left hardly any topics unexplored. I began to search for a deeper understanding to the mystery of God in an ever-broadening and deeper way. This led to my ability to hear God in ways that were surprising. God could no longer fit in a box defined by previous teachings. The truth of God is in all religious traditions even though there are different names for God and different ways to describe Him. God had always been my personal friend and, through this study, I discovered an even deeper and more intimate relationship with Him.

One afternoon, I was sitting in the doctor's waiting room when the strangest thing happened to me. I use my dreams as a way of understanding my heart and intentions. I had a dream, but it was in the daytime, and I was in a public place. All of a sudden, I lost the sense that I was in the doctor's waiting room. I was outside in the northern part of the world. Snow was everywhere but it was not snowing. It was cold but I was not cold. There was a hill covered with snow, and, to the side, a forest of trees with birch-looking tree trunks and dark-green, spruce-like leaves were also covered with snow. Out of the woods appeared the most magnificent, pure white wolf I had ever seen. His white fur glistened in the sunshine. His eyes penetrated my heart as he looked directly into mine. I felt loved, and I felt that the wolf was kind, gentle and resembled in his nature the Beloved Jesus. Without using his mouth, he began to convey a message to me. He asked me if I would go with him to a place that I had never been before. Because I felt I was in the presence of the Holy One, I said yes. When I did, I began to see sparks of light flash and dart from one tree to the next. Then into my vision came rocks, bugs, planets and people. The light reflected its spark off all these things as well. The message was that we are all connected by the essence of God and God's loving hand. Everything then became emerald green and pure blue at the same time. The beauty of each color tone was unlike anything that I have ever seen on this earth. It may be here; I just have not seen it. Then I realized that I was back in the doctor's office, sitting in the waiting room.

Where did I go? Was it just in my mind? Was it just a daydream? I have no idea. No one in the waiting room told me that I looked weird or asked me if I was all right. No time had passed. The dream had happened outside time. I called Reverend Baker, my wise friend, to ask for counsel about this experience that I will call a daydream. We discussed how things are connected. For example: letters make words, which make sentences, which make stories. The notes to music when put together make songs or symphonies. DNA put together makes creation. Trees are made of the same elements as rocks. The earth is made of the same particles that are in outer space. Hildegard of Bingen said: "We are all sparks of the Divine." The essence of God's love transforms each of us into a new creation. This newness within transforms those around us. And in transformation, we move back toward God.

Joy is connected to sorrow. Pain is connected to relief. Love is connected to hate. Every action is connected to a reaction. Everything in my life has been and will continue to be connected to every other event. Every emotion is connected to all other emotions. All persons who have moved through my life are connected to me and I to them. I am who I am because of their influence. Everything that goes out from me returns in some way. The unresolved issues in my life go out, possibly hurting others, and return in a painful way, hurting me all over again. Blessings sent out return to bless me. What choices will I make now that I have these new understandings?

Reverend Baker and I discussed the white wolf as a sacred symbol in Native American spirituality and the significance the wolf could bring into my life. The white wolf represents courage, strength, intuition, perseverance, the pathfinder, the shadow and loyalty. Reverend Baker helped me to understand this experience as a call to listen to my own true inner voice, the voice that is not ruled by what society thinks or what I think other people think. Like the wolf, I am not aggressive but can be if called upon to be. Another understanding is to know my inner power in such a way that I do not need to demonstrate it. The wolf comes out at night to howl at the moon. The moon represents my deeper, hidden side and continued exploration and verbalization will bring forth the unknown so that I may understand it. We discussed these thoughts as they related to my life's direction. I had much to ponder as I began to awaken to new possibilities.

All of life is sacred. There is no part of life that is not part of the sacred all. While some experiences are painful and perhaps degrading, they have the same overall value to the whole, as the wonderful and mysterious events and insights do. For you who have had a most devastating experience, you may be shouting in your soul: "No! That is not true. How can this that has happened to me be part of the whole? And there is no way that it is part of what was sacred!"

Each life is sacred. In my vision of the wolf, it was a surprise to me that all of life was part of the wolf himself. All life came from the essence of that magnificent animal. If the wolf is a sacred representation of the Creator God, then it follows that we are all part of creation as well. The hurtful can become the beginning of the healing process. Thus the hurtful is, with time and healing, a part of, but not the only, focus.

Reverend Baker and I concluded that the gifts of special experiences have meaning, which continues to grow as our lives unfold.

Many years later, I would move into another dark valley of the night. Each of the days of incredible pain would be connected to each other and to the deeper meaning of my life. I will always marvel at the wonder of the beauty of the wolf and my yearning to remain connected with him. Like the first encounter with the Light of Christ, I felt I was home and wanted to remain there.

As I continued my search for a deeper meaning to my life, Reverend Baker suggested that I attend the Anglican School of Theology, in Dallas, to become trained both as a spiritual director and in pastoral care. This knowledge would broaden my personal life and my professional skills. The pursuit of knowledge and the application of this new truth would, by its very nature, continue to transform me as I journeyed into all areas of my life, allowing God's light to shine on them. Spiritual direction is not about a specific religion or doctrine, but about a relationship with God.

Dolph and I had been married about a year when Mother called me for help. Dad, by his continued use of alcohol, was rapidly deteriorating. He had set the kitchen on fire attempting to cook dinner. He had caught the car on fire as he was attempting to recharge the battery. Mother and Dad lived on a private lake. Dad had waded out into the muddy part of the lake and sunk to his knees in the mud. He was unable to pull himself free. Mother placed cookie sheets end to end attempting to make a pathway for her to walk on to try to get close enough to Dad to rescue him. What kept Mother from sinking into the mud is a mystery. Both of them were eighty-four-years-old.

I remember fearing my feelings as I contemplated going to help Mother. I feared I would literally crumble into nothing if I faced the depth of my love and sadness for Mother and Dad. Nevertheless, I risked facing it. I knelt by my bed and prayed that God would hold onto me even if I shattered into little pieces. I invited God to come into the middle of the broken mess of my situation and be present as I accepted that I loved my parents. I felt an intense weight push me down toward the floor and I could do nothing but sit on the floor. While I was still in tears, the weight lifted. I could return to the kneeling position and realized I did not crack into little pieces. I was able to admit in my heart that I loved both of my parents. I had no idea how much.

I did go to be with Mother. With the help of a family physician, Dad was committed to a psychiatric hospital for detoxification. Mother discussed with Martha and me her thought that Dad needed to be placed in a nursing home once discharged from the hospital. They had been married for sixty years and had been through many struggles. However, it was Mother's call. Therefore, I honored it.

Commitment to the psychiatric hospital was to be Dad's third attempt for sobriety that I knew of. At age seventy-eight, he had gone through the Rehabilitation Center in England mainly because he had been so impressed with the way that I had been able, as the result of that treatment, to live a sober life. He had returned from England and was able to maintain sobriety for a few months. However, he returned to his choice to drink. In a weak moment, to please his family, Dad agreed to admit himself to a second rehabilitation center.

Mother had found a center in California that treated alcoholism as a dual diagnosis, alcohol abuse and depression. This second time, I escorted him, now eighty-two, to California and went through the admission process with him. Once I returned home, Dad had changed his mind and wanted someone to come back and get him. He became very angry when no one came. After three weeks, he returned home and continued to drink.

Both of us had walked the journey of alcoholism together. I felt a special closeness to him because of that. I understood his struggles and his failed attempts to gain a life of sobriety. I also felt close to him because of all of our fishing trips we had taken and our long talks. He felt especially close to me as the result of meeting me for the first time in the hotel room with the social worker so many years ago.

On his third day in the psychiatric hospital, Dad went to a hearing to decide if he had to remain there. Someone, preferably a family member, was required to testify that he needed to stay in the hospital because, if released, he would be a danger to himself or others. Since Mother emotionally was unable to go, she sent me. There are no words to describe the burden that I felt.

Committing Dad to this new psychiatric hospital, and then later to a nursing home, was a sad and painful decision. I believed that Dad might have a few healthy years left if he were able to stay sober. His drinking cohorts were not as concerned about his health as his family was.

In spite of wishing I did not have to be the family spokesperson, I went to the courtroom. The judge read the reasons why Dad had to stay in the hospital and then asked for the doctor's opinion and for mine. When I said that I agreed with the doctor—that Dad needed to stay in the hospital—he turned to me and said, *"You, too?"*

As I looked into his eyes, I could see the deep agony of betrayal that he felt. Without any more words, I felt like a knife had pierced right through my heart. I could feel the warm blood oozing out of my chest. My soul anguished for him and what he felt that I had done to him. As Dad was being taken back to his room, his head was bent down, and tears were falling down his cheeks. I felt the weight of the agony of loving him and the burden of doing what I felt was the right thing to do at the same time. Oh, dear God, I hurt!

Before Dad was released from the hospital, Mother filed for guardianship. Dad was no longer capable of making wise decisions about his health or his actions. From the hospital, Dad was moved to a nursing home. He wanted to go home. Even though Dad remained sober and began to have a life of quality and meaning, he remained angry with Mother. He would tell me he felt abandoned and his heart was broken. He was confused as to why she would not let him go home. Mother loved him deeply and I can only imagine the burden of care she carried for Dad. Most of the time it is far easier to choose what is comfortable than what is right and healthy for myself and for others. The consequences of the easy road have lasting effects that may be destructive.

A couple of years later, Mother called again to say that Dad had a stroke. He had decided to stop eating and had been hiding his medicines in his shoes without taking them. I went to the hospital to see Dad. With fear in his eyes, his first words to me were, "Is this a nuthouse place?" He had not forgotten. I, too, remembered. Because he had developed alcoholic dementia, he never understood the reasons why he was placed in the psychiatric hospital. He did not believe that his alcoholism was as critical a problem as it had been. After his health stabilized, he was returned to the nursing home and I went back to my house.

A few nights later, Mother called and said that Dad had taken a turn for the worse and to come quickly. There was a sick, empty feeling in the pit of my stomach. As I was hurriedly packing my suitcase to go to his side, I had a strong and vivid sense that Dad was standing next to me. I could feel the warmth of his body, and I thought that I felt the wind move past me as he breathed.

My spirit heard him say, "I now see my life, and understand that what I did and said hurt you. I love you and I did not mean to hurt you. I am so sorry. Will you forgive me?"

My heart felt that he fully understood and he was truly remorseful. Without hesitation I responded: "I receive your apology. I forgive you." Well, the most miraculous thing followed. It was as if a lightning ribbon (similar to the ribbon effect of the ribbon candy at Christmas) moved into my heart and pulled out all resentment, all hurts, and all residue of negative emotional pain. The memories of details remained, but the negative or painful feelings no longer had control in my heart. What we forgive on earth will be forgiven in heaven. I was set free. Love for my dad remained and a compassion for him exploded. His presence then disappeared. I later discovered that my experience was just after Dad's time of death. What happens after death remains a question. I am not a theological scholar. I just have my witness to an experience that leads me to believe there is healing in and through death for both the living and the dying.

Chapter 13

Healing of Memories

To forgive is to set a prisoner free and discover the prisoner was you.
—LEWIS B. SMEDES

As the winter of 2000 set in, so did the pain in my hip. It was not the usual kind of cold weather pain. It was more intense and took more of my energy to tolerate. I had a difficult time focusing on work and making decisions. I struggled to get through the day. My nights became restless and my body began to fatigue from lack of sleep.

That fall, Mother had discovered a lump in her breast. I took off work to take her to M. D. Anderson cancer center for an evaluation. The results of the tests verified that Mother had breast cancer and the cancer had already spread into the lymph glands. A mastectomy and the removal of the malignant lymph glands were the very minimum recommended. Chemotherapy and radiation were discussed as precautionary follow-up treatments. Mother, at eighty-six, had dedicated herself as the primary care person for Martha, who had developed MS years before. Martha's condition required assistance. Mother hired a health-care worker to provide the heavy lifting for Martha, but Mother was there twenty-four hours a day to take care of whatever my sister needed. Martha was a night owl. Her sleep pattern remained the opposite to that of Mother's. If my sister needed anything, Mother would get up and go over to Martha's home. Mother told me she had made a pledge to God, that if He would give her a baby to adopt, she would take care of him or her no matter what. Therefore, Mother labored in her self-giving. She was worn out from the physical schedule she was keeping. She was worried about Chad, who still lived in her home, and spent hours thinking of ways that she could help him put his life together in a meaningful way. Her burdens were heavy.

In her minimal amount of spare time, Mother played the piano, was actively involved in her church and social groups, and cared for all of her plants. She lived a life of service to others, and it was difficult for her to receive help.

Mother wanted to retain the quality of her life, so she therefore refused chemotherapy. She was also concerned that having a mastectomy would interfere with her ability to play the piano but she reluctantly agreed to have surgery. To combat her fears, she increased her piano practice time. Mother was grieving deeply about her condition. She held in her feelings until she could put her grief into words. The diagnosis of cancer was very, very sad news for us. It is difficult to be told that someone you love has cancer. We were all grieving in our own ways. We talked about her concerns and we cried. We talked about options and consequences. A relationship with her, deeper than I ever dreamed possible, was beginning to develop for me. Mother began to humbly verbalize her feelings to me.

After my adoption search, alcohol recovery and college, Mother and I had begun to develop a meaningful friendship. I was able to accept that her goals for my life were noble. She wanted me to develop all the talents that were available to me. She wanted me to have character, culture and style. She wanted me to be educated. She wanted me to attain a happy and successful life. Her behaviors that I once resented were diminishing in power. I was able to just let them go. I noticed she was being more forthcoming with praise and attention. Her counsel seemed to have wisdom I needed to hear. As our relationship began to deepen, I wanted to explore the possibility there might be any remaining emotional wounds. I decided to go for therapy because I wanted to identify those areas and find healing before Mother became too ill for us to talk about them. The problem I carried in my relationship to her was in my reaction to her based on my misperceptions and on my unmet needs. She loved me; however, I could not accept it. I spent so much time blinded by my abandonment issues that I lost the opportunity to receive her love.

I stayed in therapy for a year, addressing my many negative beliefs. I had believed that she loved my sister more than me based on her seeming approval of my sister and her disapproval of me. After reviewing the facts, I found this belief to be false. Mother loved us differently but equally. One other problem that I will mention here was my relationship with my former husband. I believed that he was unable to emotionally nurture me within the marriage. In and after the divorce, I raged against him for his lack of caring about his own children as well. He did not listen to me while we were married, and he had continued that pattern with his children. I had not dealt with my divorce, my anger with him, and all the unmet needs that I had felt. It was a very painful journey to go into, seeing my part in the failing relationship. With increased understanding, I was able to claim 100 percent of my half of the failure. Even with claiming responsibility, I was unable to forgive David.

One day, as I was listening to the radio, I heard Willie Nelson singing his wonderful song, "You Were Always On My Mind," and I had an awakening.

As Willie sang the words, *I'm so sorry I was blind*, my heart heard my former husband's voice, instead of Willie Nelson's, say those words. I suddenly believed that David did not understand what was happening to me and I received an apology from his spirit. As I melted into tears with my own deep heartfelt remorse for my part, I was set free from the burden of resentment. I was able to see that I had given to him the job of taking care of my needs and that was not his responsibility. I realized that I missed him so much; I missed what could have been had things been different. Just like accepting my father's apology after his death, there were no hurt feelings about David that continued to live in me. What freedom! What a lesson! Above all, what a miraculous blessing!

The healings continued as I began to see my mother from a new perspective within my heart. Each time I went into the depth of my hurts, I was challenged to face the wounding in myself, challenged to forgive her and to see how I had also hurt her. The journey inward was painful. The emotional pain intensified the physical pain. I wept often. As I began to see the big picture of her life and my relationship with her, I began to love her for who she was and not push her love away. I came to understand that her intentions were noble, even though I had been wounded. She loved me and did the very best that she could at being my mother. As my heart continued to heal, I began to remember the blessings she gave to me. I began to remember times when she did care for me. I remembered actions of compassion. I remembered times when she was nurturing. I remembered that she loved me. My love and respect for her grew and became the blessing that allowed me to be fully present for her through her illness.

Chapter 14

DEATH AND RESURRECTION

*Goodbyes are only for those who love with their eyes.
Because for those who love with heart and soul
there is no such thing as separation.*

—RUMI

Before mother's surgery, I went to my orthopedic surgeon to inquire about this new kind of pain in my hip. Usually in the winter, my hip would flare with arthritic pain. However, this year, the pain was more intense than it ever had been. I had begun to drag the leg since it was too painful for me to pick it up to walk. I could not sleep. I became easily irritated. To minimize the pain, I had to increase my fidgeting movements. It was almost impossible to sit in the therapy room for an hour, listening intently to my clients. My pain was nagging for attention. After another x-ray at the doctor's office, I was told that it was time for a revision of the hip replacement. The top half of the total hip hardware was deteriorating rapidly. The doctor and I discussed my situation concerning my mother and I received permission to postpone surgery for as long as the doctor felt was safe. He recommended I use a cane to minimize the weight on the hip. I followed his instructions and bought a cane. The next morning I attended a continuing education workshop leaning on my cane. I found that I could not use the cane, hold my purse, and get the coffee or sweets that were being offered at the workshop. I almost burst into tears. A deep sadness, covered with disappointment, came over me and I felt so alone. So many old memories flooded back into my heart. I did not hear much of the workshop presentation. I had gone internal with my thoughts. I was losing my sense of independence as my sense of vulnerability was increasing.

I made many trips to Mother's house to take her back and forth to M. D. Anderson. On her first visit, the doctors suspected breast cancer. Repeated visits and many tests gave the doctors the information they needed to make a diagnosis...breast cancer. We discussed her options. She chose surgery but no chemo. She wanted quality of life for the life she had left. My heart grieved for all the other patients there and for what they were facing. I cried for Mother and her struggles. I began to notice that Mother was changing more and more to resemble a little child. This insight triggered my motherly instinct. I became very protective of her. As a mother would have compassion for her child, I was aware that I had a similar compassion for Mother. The blessing arose when Mother and I began to talk about the true essences of life. We developed a mother-daughter relationship that I previously had dreamed about but never dared to think was possible.

The day of Mother's breast surgery, we went together to the hospital. A mastectomy was only a twenty-three-hour stay in the hospital. When discharged she would return home where she would have home health care for her wound. Mother was hurting emotionally as she faced the unknown. She was carrying the burden of caring for my sister and my brother. Mother was not sure she would recover her strength to continue assisting with my sister's care. She was also concerned whether she would be able to play her piano after surgery. And more than any of these, I was hurting emotionally for her and all that she was facing. I was in excruciating physical pain. I would break out in sweats as I attempted to move from one place to another. I found myself shaking with the intensity of the pain. It was almost impossible for me to focus on anything other than my pain. I needed supernatural energy to focus on Mother and what she was experiencing rather than on me. By God's grace, I was able to put my needs aside.

The pain medication did not seem to be successful in relieving Mother's post-surgery pain. She seemed to be mumbling about her leg hurting. When I inquired about it, she was able, through the fog of medication, to tell me about a traumatic event in her life that had injured her leg and ended with the death of her horse. Once she could acknowledge the event and the feeling of sadness associated with it, the pain subsided. She went peacefully to sleep. What a miracle! Even though she was in physical pain, no medication was needed. All that was required was for her to acknowledge the event. As I have said before, physical pain and emotional pain are intertwined and the body often feels the agony of both without differentiation.

There was no rest from my pain, however. On a scale from one to ten, the pain level was about nine-and-a-half. It was hard for me to separate the emotional from the physical pain. Mother's surgery revealed the cancer had spread into all the lymph nodes and into the chest cavity. Radiation would buy time but time was running out sooner than we had hoped.

Mother said she did not want me to be sad. We had done all we could and it just had not been soon enough. She did not want me to blame myself. I guess she knew that I would. After Mother's stitches were removed, I returned to my home and to work. My brother agreed to take mother back and forth to radiation therapy three times a week. It was very uncomfortable for Mother and she complained of pain. I would drive down to her home on weekends. With each visit I could see that she was becoming weaker. She was losing her hair and her motivation to play the piano.

I changed from using a cane to using crutches as I continued to postpone my surgery date. Finally, my doctor said I could not wait any longer. By now I was totally non-weight-bearing and using the assistance of crutches. The upper-half of the original hip replacement had worn thin and I was in danger of the femur bone protruding into the pelvic cavity. Therefore, the doctor insisted I schedule the surgery. As I have previously mentioned, the initial total hip replacement had been glued in. The doctor told me that in order for him to put in a partial revision (only the top half of the initial total hip replacement, called an acetabular cup), he needed to scrape the old one out from the bone. He said that good bone also was destroyed. Not until he had opened me up would he be able to tell how much damage to the healthy bone had occurred. Cadaver bone chips from the bone bank were used as bone grafts to fill in the spaces. The pelvic bone was paper-thin and the doctor said that he could have put his finger through to the internal organs. Had I waited any longer for surgery, the thighbone most probably would have pushed through the pelvic cavity and into the internal organs, causing life-threatening damage. After the surgery, I rejoiced that there had been no such internal damage and I recovered as planned. I went to rehab to strengthen the muscles.

The rehabilitation physician's assistant admitted me into the rehab program. I did not see the doctor until discharged. I wondered at the time if my rehabilitation plan was specific to the need to be cautious because of the bone grafts. I trusted the process, but I still wondered. I remember one night during rehab. My roommate liked to keep the TV and the lights on all night. I cannot sleep with either in the room. I was in pain and my tolerance for such nuisances was nil. I asked the nurse to assist me in having my roommate turn them off. The nurse did turn them both off. My roommate woke up and was angry and demanded that they be turned back on. Back on they went! When the nurse left, I gathered my blanket and pillow balancing them on my walker and rolled into the bathroom, turned out the light and closed the door behind me. It was tricky to get to the floor without touching my right leg on the floor. I managed. In the bathroom, I could control the noise and the light. The next morning the nurse found me and was horrified. She quickly found me another room and I was transferred before breakfast. I spend my days exercising and getting stronger. I was to remain on a walker with minimal pressure on my right leg for another six weeks. Pain levels began to decrease and my energy was returning.

Two weeks after my surgery, Mother had a seizure and almost died. She was taken to the hospital where her doctor told the family that Mother now had a brain tumor and that she had less than six weeks to live. Why no one had mentioned the possibility of a brain tumor to us before is a mystery. Mother might not have gone through either the surgery or the radiation therapy. All she had asked for was some quality of life for the time that she had left. Be that as it may, the doctor placed her in hospice care and sent her home to die. I went to her home to be with her. Both Martha and Chad waited until I was there so that I could tell Mother about her medical status. The role I had been given as the family's emotional "fixer" continued. It is hard to shake the long-established roles that are assigned to family members. All of us were grieving, and this was beyond difficult for me. How do you say to someone you love: "The cancer has taken over your body and there is nothing else the doctors can do"? There is no way to prepare for such a task.

I felt overwhelmed with my own grief. My emotions were stronger than my ability to put into words what I wanted to say. I was not ready to begin the end journey of letting go of her. With a prayer for wisdom and a heaviness of heart, I gathered all the courage and compassion I could find and went to her. I cried as I told her and she cried as she listened. She did not want to die. She said that she still had much unfinished business. We planned the business she could do while she felt like it. Cousins came from out of town to see her, her friends at the church came to pray with her, she made phone calls, and I wrote letters for her. She took rides in the car to see the flowers or stop for ice cream. She played the piano and listened to music. We hired twenty-four-hour care, since none of us was physically able to lift her. The brain tumor began to cause Mother more disorientation, forgetfulness and pain. The cancer in her lymph system and moving into the bones in her rib cage was growing rampant and causing great pain. To make matters worse, Mother got the shingles. She was on three kinds of pain medication: for the cancer in her bones, for shingles (nerve) and for brain swelling. Her eyes told me she was still in some degree of pain even with all of her medications. Soon she could not swallow her medication; medicated cream was applied to the skin and injections were given as needed.

Martha would roll over in her electric wheelchair from her home next door for daily visits. She would bring music on tapes and play them for Mother. Chad was there to run errands when needed. Being present in the end of a loved one's life has the potential for healing, awe and wonder for the overall plan of life. Mother had many memories that would surface and we would talk about them. She told me about places, events, and people in her life about which I had never known. I did not know that Mother had been first (violin) chair/conductor of her high school symphony. She organized an orchestra of teen musicians from all over the US to go to New York and play on the Queen Mary ocean liner. A short movie clip was being filmed and Mother was filmed conducting the teen orchestra. We giggled and cried together. I was able to tell her how much I loved her and how grateful I was to her and Dad for adopting me. They had given me experiences and opportunities that had helped me to develop into the person I had become. I forgot I was recovering from surgery. My physical pain had diminished and serving Mother seemed to change my focus. My suffering was minuscule compared to Mother's. Six weeks went by too quickly.

On the morning of what was to be her last day, a rainbow appeared that stretched across the sky and landed in the middle of her lake. The view could be seen from the window near Mother's bed, which was in her living room next to her piano. Rainbows have the awesome symbolism of witnessing to God's faithfulness to His word and to His steadfast promises of His love. It was only as evening time rolled around that we understood the special gift of the rainbow on that day.

As Mother's blood pressure dropped and the signs of immediate death presented, I wanted more time. Please wait! Do not die yet! There was so much I wanted to say. I prayed that time would stand still. I found that indeed time did seem to slow down, almost to a standstill. I thought I saw an exact image of Mother's fragile body hovering just above her. Her physical body had substance while the other was more transparent, airy and light. It did not seem to have weight and therefore was floating. I wondered if I were seeing Mother's soul. From her floating image, her eyes were looking intensely at me as though trying to say something. Was I witnessing her soul as it was leaving her body to go to Heaven? I became frozen as I watched this mystery. At the time, I wondered if I was fabricating the vision in my grief. Possibly, my double vision from dyslexia was playing tricks on me or actually serving as a blessing for me at this time. Maybe it was real. If it was real, what did it mean? Was Mother teaching me about what is beyond the grave? As I sat quietly with her holding her hand, she slipped peacefully away along with the transparency. In peace and at rest, she let out her last breath.

There was a beauty in her death at her own home. There were no loud instruments going off, no medical staff needing to check in for vital signs, and we had all the time we needed before she had to be taken to the funeral home. Martha, Chad and I sat next to her bed and we remembered her with laughter and tears. A sense of her presence remained for days. The priest came and gave her a blessing, and then a good friend came with the funeral home personnel to ride to the funeral home. Above all, Mother was in her favorite room in her home, with a view of the lake outside and near to her beloved piano.

A few days after the funeral, I returned home. I had been given the task of closing Mother's estate and, therefore, there were tons of boxes with paperwork to go through. The boxes full of documents seemed endless.

Due to the situation with Mother, I had missed the normal six-week, follow-up, post-surgery visit with my surgeon. By the time I could make the visit, I had begun to notice a strange click when I walked or moved. I mentioned this to the surgeon and, after he examined me, he ordered an x-ray. *Yuk!* The new hardware in the hip had cracked loose from the bone grafts, which had cracked loose from my body. Two of the many screws that had been put in to hold the new hardware had broken. I had to have surgery again to replace the damage.

No! This was not fair! Why me? I must be dreaming! The doctor must have looked at someone else's pictures! What happened? Maybe it was the doctor's fault? Were the bone grafts not compatible with my body so that I thus had rejected the transplant? Was the orthopedic surgeon incompetent? A failed replacement! Had rehab been too strenuous? The rehab doctor never examined me so maybe his rehab regime was the culprit. Where was God? My prayer team had prayed for blessings and health to be the outcome from that surgery. We had even prayed for guidance about God's will for which orthopedic surgeon to choose. Had he answered my prayer with a failed surgery? Why would God be responsible for a failed surgery? If He had not answered my prayers, why not?

Did He even care? And now, after the death of Mother, I had to go through all of this again!

My heart was so heavy. I felt betrayed by the surgeon, by the rehabilitation doctor and by God. I had to start recovery all over again. I was not sure if I could stand another surgery. There would be more trauma to the muscles and to the bones. I was confused. I was outraged. I had a hodgepodge of feelings all jumbled up in my heart. I was so disappointed and outraged that I cried and cried and cried.

Chapter 15

EXAMPLE OF BROKENNESS

For something to be great, there has to be some kind of trial or some type of struggle that actually makes it special or valuable to you. Otherwise, anything could be easily taken for granted.
—HAYLEY WILLIAMS

I scheduled the surgery date a month away. I felt like I needed to work and have some time to attend to some of the business of my mom's estate. Dolph took me back and forth to Mother's home to get the boxes and boxes of files that I needed to settle her affairs and I began the preliminary cleaning out of her home. We were going to have to sell the home and the property that had belonged to my grandfather to pay the estate taxes. The system is so unfair. My family had already paid taxes on the value of the property and to have to sell now was, in my opinion, a crime.

It was incredibly sad. My grandfather bought the home with acreage when I was about two years old. Originally, a log cabin with a magnificent rock fireplace rising from the floor in the living room was on the property. My grandfather added two bedrooms. We would go there on weekends to get away from the business of city life. We would have so much fun! We would ride horses and take long walks in the forest. There was a lake on the property where Dad and I would go fishing. He enjoyed taking me out in the rowboat. Dad and I developed a special relationship as we experienced these activities together. Martha and I would find a special spot for the family to say Sunday morning prayers.

Being back in Mother and Dad's home after her death brought up such sadness in my heart. The empty house felt strange. I did not hear her music. I did, however, sense her presence. The air was heavy. The brown-stained Mexican tile floor was cold to walk on. The beautiful lake that had once been vibrant with wildlife and sunbeams seemed to have lost its luster. Mother loved the lake and the memory of this remains but her energy of love was gone. I missed my mother's presence. I couldn't smell her perfume nor was there any music being made on her piano. My brother, sister and I sat quietly listening to the silence hoping to hear Mother's voice again. But the house was hauntingly quiet. There were to be no more new memories, no more Christmases, no more learning about her. The more that I missed her, the more my hip hurt. The more my hip hurt, the more my sadness about having to have surgery grew. I was so disappointed. We did sell the home, and immediately the new owner, without regard to the trees, clear-cut this beautiful property. The one-hundred-and-fifty acres were now flat and barren, which is how I felt whenever I thought about Mother, which was often. When I thought about her now butchered property, I felt like I had betrayed her.

When my second surgery was over, I chose to go home rather than to a rehabilitation facility. There was more pain after the surgery than before. Because of the trauma of the repeated surgery itself, I was suffering badly. I did not like the new bone grafts. I emotionally was at odds with "something" internally. I could not define it. My doctor told me that he did not know of any reason why my body would reject the grafts. Maybe it was healing and I just was unable to properly identify what my body felt. I did not like the feelings that I had. The scar tissue was tightening and causing burning pain. The sciatic nerve must have been compromised in surgery (a listed side effect), thus the continued searing pain in my back, down my leg and into my foot. I was awake most nights, pacing the floor with my walker, shaking in pain and crying my heart out.

One of the ways that I helped my body tolerate pain was to move around. I was only able to use toe-touch weight-bearing with the walker. Therefore, it was not possible to reduce the pain with movement. Nighttime was so quiet in our apartment. I was emotionally and physically exhausted and feeling panicked about not being able to sleep. I heard all the sounds of the traffic passing by. I heard the neighbors talking outside their homes. I smelled the food from the restaurant across the street. I turned off the lights in the hopes that I would psychologically believe it was time to sleep. But I could not rest.

I moved around in the cold dark night. God had come to me in the night once before. Where was He now? I hurt seemingly beyond my ability to tolerate the pain. My husband was sound asleep. We had talked about what he could do and we had accepted there really was nothing that would be helpful. He wanted to protect me from all the agony that I was experiencing, but he could not. I love him for trying everything that he could think of to ease my pain. Even as he accepted his limitations, he still grieved for me. He had loved my mother, too, and was grieving her loss at the same time with me. The doctor tried many different kinds of pain medications including muscle relaxants and nerve medications; none provided relief. Even the sheets on the bed caused excruciating pain. The fiery pain felt like I was being burned alive.

During the day, I would go through my mother's files reading all the different things that she had stored there. Mother had a box marked "treasures." In it were memories that were very special to her. I found pictures of friends, old classmates and family. There were old letters from her friends and her family and old Mother's Day and birthday cards from loved ones. I found her favorite Bible verses and sermons. As I went through and read each item, I grieved my loss over and over again. I missed her so badly. I wanted to talk to her about what each item had meant to her and learn more about her. My heart hurt terribly during the day and my leg hurt tremendously at night. Deep sadness would sweep over me at unpredictable times and catch me unprepared. I cried interminably. Grief is truly the deepest of the human emotions. I did not know if I would ever stop grieving her.

Going through the box of her treasures, I found cards and letters from me that did express my love and appreciation for her.

> *Grief is truly the deepest of the human emotions.*

I had forgotten all about these mementos. Over the last several years I had discovered that my love for her had been buried under an illusion that led to my rejection of her. It had been important to me that she knew I loved her before she died. I could now accept she knew, in spite of my behavior, that I loved her. A sense of healing washed over me and I knew the grieving process was healing me. A special insight born in my deep grieving for Mother was the idea that God feels grief, deeper than what I was experiencing for Mother, for His children when we turn away from Him. I am reminded of the scripture passage when Jesus says: "O Jerusalem, Jerusalem… How often would I have gathered your children together as a hen gathers her brood under her wings, and you would not." (Matthew 23:37, RSV). Really, the entire story of God, as written in the Old and New Testaments, is a love story of His passionate attempts to reach out to His people. Years later, I still miss her. I smell her perfume, I hear her voice, I remember the funny things, and I laugh as well as cry. The thought that came to me was that my grief was testimony to my deep love for her. Perhaps I had underestimated the strength of our bond?

In my grief, I felt excruciating physical pain. I began to ask my body if the pain that I was feeling was physical or emotional. When I could determine which, I would medicate accordingly. This seemed to be the answer for me. If it was physical, I took the prescribed medication; if emotional, I would sit and grieve until the pain softened. The pain medication made me sleepy and I did not like to take it during the day for that reason. But, having been up all night in tears from the intensity of pain, I found that sleep was good. I liked the way the hydrocodone curbed the pain, heightened my mind and gave me energy. However, continuing it past my time of pain was not even contemplated.

After two months of recovery from my surgery, I was able to put full weight on my leg. The muscles were not strong enough to tolerate my full body weight, which made it necessary to continue to use a cane. I returned to work. The pain medication made me sleepy; therefore, I chose not to take the level of medication needed to stop the pain. As a psychotherapist, I needed to be alert.

A strange phenomenon began to develop. Because I was still in great pain, which could be seen in my eyes, and I was struggling with my cane, my clients felt a special connection to my suffering. Many of the walls that my clients built as protection to hide behind came down. They reported feeling that, because of my suffering, I would understand theirs. I believe the walls that separate a therapist from the client were blurred significantly. For most of my clients, my suffering triggered their compassion and they wanted to connect to me by sharing their pain. I felt honored to be allowed to move with them so deeply into their hearts.

As time passed, my frustration with the pain increased. I began to wonder if I had cause to sue the surgeon or possibly the rehabilitation doctor. The rehab doctor never really examined me; it was his physician's assistant who initiated the rehab program. I sought legal counsel. The lawyer said that he had several claims already filed against the rehabilitation doctor for malpractice and my case should be investigated. I seriously considered his counsel. I remembered some of my clients, who through their own pursuit of legal remediation for wrongful medical intervention, became embittered as they also became obsessed with the process. I decided that, even if I were justified in my claims of malpractice by either the orthopedic surgeon or the physical medicine doctor, or both, I would not pursue legal action. I was already struggling with such difficulty to heal that becoming consumed with anger would only interfere further with my healing process.

I was losing my belief that God answers prayers. I prayed for answers. I prayed for the cessation of pain. I prayed for help. I became angry with God. Who was God, anyway? Why was He so cruel to allow me to hurt with such intensity or for so long? I had been through enough. What kind of God would answer some prayers and not others? I forgot the long history of God's blessings in my life. I forgot that He has always answered my prayers in His time and in His way to secure His outcome. I was surprised how quickly

I forgot that He is interested in healing my spiritual life as well as my physical or emotional life. Under the heavy weight of the pain I was enduring physically and mentally, I forgot that God does indeed care about me. I forgot He sees the big picture and I see only a very tiny speck of it.

The longevity and the intensity of pain wore me down and I became disheartened. I became discouraged about my situation. I lost hope that things would ever get any better. The pain was all consuming and it infiltrated every fiber of my being. I was irritable toward my husband and did not want to be touched. If he wanted to talk about what was on my mind, I wanted to withdraw. His ability to tolerate the changes in my response to him, because I hurt so badly, was a gift of grace. One of my friends said to me: "what you are experiencing is a stressful situation, and you *should* be glad that it is not an illness. This situation has a solution." While the intent of my friend was to provide comfort, those words just added to the intensity of my pain and sadness. I felt broken and unable to function. I felt I had lost my ability to hold on to a God who answered prayers. I felt absorbed in self-focus because my needs were not quickly resolved. These answers were not happening my way or in my time.

My depression led to my inability to push through the pain with the drive that I once had. There were days that I did not want to get out of bed and go to work. I would pull the covers up over my head and say: "I am not doing this today." And yet, I was pulled to reach out to the pain of others. I would get up and go to work, unable to hide the physical pain that I was experiencing. My clients saw, in my eyes and in the way I walked, that I was in unbearable pain, and thus were assured that I would understand their pain. They identified my brokenness with their pain. They could relate to me, risk being open and accept the real possibility of being helped.

A special blessing came from one of the ministers in my church who had cerebral palsy. He is both physically and verbally challenged. One Sunday, not yet able to kneel, I was standing at the altar rail with my hands outstretched waiting to receive communion from him. As the broken minister placed the communion bread into my hands, I heard the words, which seemed to be coming from Jesus himself, say: "I am broken *for* you; you are broken *with* me." I felt an overwhelming sense of holiness in my brokenness, oneness with Jesus and with the minister. Healing was not physical at that moment. The healing was deeper than words, for it moved me into a place of acceptance for my brokenness as a blessing. My soul became softer as a result, and the power of that moment was not disabling, but rather, strong, upright and unlimited. Healing is a promise from God. It comes in many unexpected ways.

Chapter 16

Healing with Dreams and Other Blessings

*The dream shows the inner truth and reality of the
individual as it really is: not as I conjecture it to be, and
not as he or she would like it to be, but as it is.*

—CARL JUNG

In my own struggles in recovery, I have learned much about pain, setbacks, body image, other people's reactions to the disabled, feeling abandoned by God and prayers answered not in the way I had asked for. I have faced the stark truth that I abandoned God. I have found that there were times in which I wanted to pull the covers up over my head and not face the day. There were times when those closest to me were more of a thorn in my side than a comfort. I have struggled with depression, disappointment, disillusionment, doubt and loss of what was part of me. I have experienced the fear that nothing was going to get any better and the fear that the pain and the limitations I was experiencing would always be with me. I have been angry and resentful. I have wrestled with why God chose to leave me crippled.

If I look at the meaning of all that I was experiencing and thinking, I realize that the healing of my leg also involved the healing of the whole self. Not only my ability to walk, but to walk upright in personal truth—truth that gave me the strength and allowed me to walk in and over treacherous terrain through the storms of life symbolically as well as literally. I was challenged to look into the other non-physical ways I was crippled. Could I trust even in the midst of the dark night of my soul? Could I allow life's experiences to take the necessary shape, so that empathy to relate to others in a deeper awareness of love might be born in my heart? Could I break that I might assist others in being set free?

> *Could I trust even in the midst of the dark night of my soul?*

A few years after I retired from a career as a psychotherapist, I began a new adventure as an author and a photographer. The years following have been an incredible adventure in seeing, through the lenses of the camera, the beautiful and mysterious world that God has made. I published a book that combines my photography and text relating to the meaning of dream symbols. I have published a book entitled *Lives*

Interrupted: The Unwanted Pregnancy Dilemma. And there will certainly be more books in the future.

Although I am a self-taught photographer, professional photographers George DeWolfe, Craig Varjabedian and my husband, Dolph, have influenced my style of photography through their critique and their philosophy about techniques, lighting and being present to the space that is being photographed. The creative processes of photography, dream symbolism and writing a memoir, all come from the same source, the muse within.

To learn more, I attended workshops. It was both fun to see through the eye of the camera and to begin to see detail in life as never before. What challenged my nerves was at the end of each workshop; the instructor presented a slideshow of photographs from the participants. Ugh! I rarely thought mine were worthy of show-and-tell. If the stress was more than I could cope with at the time, I would refuse to allow my photographs to be shown. At one show-and-tell, the instructor was slightly more insistent that I explain to the group why I took that photograph and why I developed it the way I did than any other instructor I had had. As I attempted to explain myself, I drew blanks of thought and my throat was began to tighten. Public shame overpowered me and I was using all my energy to keep from bursting into tears and running out of the room. When the session was over, I did go back to my room and fall apart. The pain of humiliation and shame was more real than I could ever imagine that it had been. Each time these old wounds reappear, it is an opportunity to look at the issue again and from a deeper level.

The muse yearned to speak and to be known. She has hounded me until I answered her call. The Muse challenged me to intuitively see my world from a nonlinear perspective. I like to see and to understand reality in a clear and definable form. The Muse invited me into mystery without form or limits. I was very uncomfortable. I was restless and had trouble focusing on this mystery. Old discarded memories of inadequacy and public embarrassment arose, attempting to take up residence in my mind again. I questioned if I would ever be permanently separated from their power. Childhood impressions are deeply implanted and from time to time reappear.

My photography mentors asked me to define my photography voice. I had no idea what they meant. I explored other famous photographers and artists looking for a style I gravitated toward. I was apprehensive about setting my own style as I thought I had to photograph in a certain way. I found myself mimicking my husband's style. Once I understood that by impersonating someone else's work, I was presenting a false self, I sought a creativity coach to help me discover my own voice. Gradually, I began to trust that I was made as a creative being. Just like the rest of my uniqueness, my expression of creativity was a gift to be celebrated.

I love to travel this gorgeous and magnificent land and to see that the beautiful designs that the creator has painted are rare gifts. The photographs that I am able to bring home are exceptional treasures. I find it energizing to digitally render them on the computer and I delight in the playfulness I have when I change the photograph to look abstract or keep it realistic. The creative spirit within finds its life and new potential as I give it permission to be expressive. So now when I photograph, it is a celebration of wonder and spontaneity.

The symbolic language of dreams became a fascination and I wanted to go out and photograph them. Many synchronistic happenings began to show up. For example, I had been dreaming of spiders and toy trains. I went looking for images to photograph. Spiders were easy but the toy train was nowhere to be found. The next weekend my husband and I went to a nearby town to browse through the art district and to photograph at a botanical garden. At one of the art shops, I saw a piece of pottery that was hanging on the wall. I reached for it and took it off the wall. A Brown Recluse spider from the back of the pottery crawled down my arm and fell to the floor. Then on to the gardens we went. On the way out, there was a toy train designed with an elaborate city the train ran through. What did these symbols mean? A whole new journey was born.

The symbolic language of dreams became a fascination and I wanted to go out and photograph them.

I sought the advice of a spiritual director to help me understand what all of this might mean for me and what God might be revealing to me through these questions and symbols. I was torn between the obvious presence of God's blessings in my therapy office and the incredible lingering agony of pain which often seemed to me as if God had abandoned me.

In the process of this search, working with a spiritual director, I had two more dreams that are meaningful. The psychoanalyst, Carl Jung, used dreams to help in the healing process with his clients. Many cultures have also used dreams for revelation. Dreams are a natural source for understanding the subconscious. As Shakespeare writes in *The Tempest* (IV, i): "We are such stuff as dreams are made on, and our little life is rounded with a sleep." Our dreams are made from our own stories and have meaning for us. Dreams that provide healing and offer warnings are documented in the Bible. Our memories are our experiences and they shape and guide us every minute of the day. And our dreams are a reflection of those memories that linger below the surface.

My dreams are usually composed of a series of images, actions, words, thoughts and feelings over which I have little or no conscious control. The people, places and things of my dreams can sometimes be related to remembered life experiences or images that remain in my memory. However, more often they seem to come from sources to which I have little or no conscious access. I believe that we all dream even if we do not remember those dreams. I believe that our dreams are gifts to help us understand our journey in life. Understanding our dreams takes writing them down and working with them to decode their meaning. If I tried to ignore the inner world, as most of us do, the unconscious found its way into my life through pathology: as in physical complaints, compulsions and emotional stress.

In the first dream that I want to share, I am climbing down into a canyon similar to the Grand Canyon. Down deep I climb, and when I reach the bottom, it is a flat valley. No trees or greenery are present. There is a running stream with light refracting off the water as it rushes over the rocks. There is so much light dancing off the water that it looks as if I am looking into the heavens at night and seeing all the stars. The banks on either side of the stream are wide, brown-dirt pathways with rocks along the trail. Then the ground rises dramatically upward setting the boundaries of the canyon walls and exposing all the colors and configurations of the layers of the earth that have formed over the eons of time. I start walking peacefully along the well-worn path by the riverbank. Then suddenly, out of nowhere, stands a big brown bear on his hind feet; his arms are outstretched, and his claws are extended. His teeth are exposed as he snarls loudly at me.

I say to him: "What are *you* doing here? Be quiet!" To my surprise, the bear obeys and returns to all four feet on the ground. The bear becomes docile. He looks at me lovingly and we then walk along the riverbank together. I feel the brown hair on his back as I move my hand over him. I see the light shining off the hair follicles. We are at peace with one another. We are friends and cojourneymen as we walk along together. We walk for a while and then I awake.

What might this dream mean for me as I struggled to make sense of the pain I was experiencing, the disappointment that surgery had not been successful, my guilt for possibly choosing the wrong doctor and my crisis of faith? I was extremely worried that the pain would never stop. My life was actually consumed with pain. I was paranoid that I might hurt worse. I became very overprotective of where I would go and how closely I would stand next to others. I reacted to any threat of pain like someone with post-traumatic stress disorder. I feared that it would occur even without any real present danger. At just the thought that it could get worse, I would shake with anxiety. On days that the pain increased, I would sink into disappointment that seemed too heavy for me to carry.

I considered, as a possible interpretation of this dream, that the things I fear or find anxiety-provoking could be my friends. I would need to face them squarely and confront them. I felt a sense of empowerment to take action once again. Anxiety could be my friend. Pain could be my friend. I remembered the instruction of my cousin from my childhood "to embrace the pain." It was harder to embrace it now because of the length of time I have been in pain. But, I could do it.

The second dream that I want to share is about a lion. I am in a dungeon-like cave, waiting to be devoured by a lion as punishment for what I believe to be true. I will not deny my belief, and I am going to be the lion's dinner because of my steadfastness. The lion comes into the dungeon and walks over to me. He is magnificently beautiful. He is powerful in stature. I know that death is imminent. I surrender to the pain of such a torturous end and accept that my time to die has come. The lion stands for a while, looking at me lovingly and then turns and walks back toward the door. Some men rush into the dungeon and start beating the lion with sticks. The lion does not resist. As the lion begins bleeding, he falls to his knees. He turns his head toward me and seems to say: "I love you."

My heart cries out: "It should be me dying. You have given your life for me. Why me?" The only answer is: "I love you."

The multiple meanings of this dream will continue to unfold as my life unfolds. As a beginning, the dream might mean that I fear standing up for my truth out of fear of being destroyed. The dream indicates the possibility that I am not destroyed. There is also the idea that it is a remembrance of the story of Christ and His sacrifice for me. This sacrifice evokes selfless giving. It is also a humble reminder that I am loved. It is a blessing for me to know that there is no limit to which God will go to show me. I could imagine that God must grieve for us as He yearns for us to respond to His loving us. His heart must break when we do not respond to His seeking us for a relationship. In all my forgetfulness, God remains faithful. In all my denying that God is involved, He remains faithful. In all my fear, God is there. In all the times that I abandon Him, he remains true. God shares my pain. He walks with me wherever I go and there is nothing that can separate me from Him. Nothing!

Another thought was that the lion symbolically represented me. The lion's (my alter ego) task was to destroy my decision to stand firm on my truths. The lion decided not to destroy the truth. He decided to allow the truth to live in exchange for his death. The important fact here is I am acceptable as I am.

My fear of pain and the lack of hope that anything would ever be different shifted focus. I could embrace the pains in my life and I would not be destroyed. In fact, I would be liberated by my acceptance.

In late September of 2002, as I leaned over to pick something up off the floor, I felt and heard a crack. Oh no! *Not again!* This could not be! No injury, no overexertion, and nothing to stress the hip, so what was happening? It was too easy for the hip to break loose. Maybe it had never attached successfully. A trip to the orthopedic doctor showed upon x-ray that the second hip revision had indeed broken loose.

I almost had a sense of relief. It seemed strange that although I was tremendously disappointed that I would have to go through another surgery, I was also glad that a third time might allow my leg to "feel" right in my body. I had carried around a sense that the second hip was out of sync with my body. The bone graft *felt* wrong, the muscles did not want to walk with a normal rhythm and I hurt most of the time. I still had to walk with a cane due to the pain. I had hoped to be able to resume a lifestyle that would allow me to hike, to carry my own tray at a cafeteria or to put the laundry away. My loss of independence had remained. The list of losses went on and on. So many simple things are taken for granted until they are gone.

Before the surgery for the first revision, I had tried to find Doctor Joe King, the orthopedic surgeon, who had performed my original hip replacement, but was unable to locate him. I knew the town, but there was no listing in his name. It had been thirty years and I suspected that he was deceased. My brother asked his cardiologist if he knew of an excellent orthopedic surgeon who specialized in failed hip replacements. His doctor suggested the Fondren Clinic in Houston. I called and asked the receptionist for the name of the doctor at the clinic who specialized in failed hip replacements. I was transferred to a nurse. After a brief description of my situation, she made an appointment for me to see the doctor. With great hope, I went to the appointment.

There in the lobby of the Fondren Orthopedic Clinic was a large picture of *Dr. Joe King,* founder of the Fondren Clinic. My mercy, what a blessing has been given to me! What a big surprise! It was like God was shouting: "I heard your prayers and I sent you here." God had been in the middle of my physical pain and in my spiritual and emotional distress. He had not abandoned me. I had an overwhelming sense that this surgery would be successful and that everything was going to be all right. Moreover, it was.

I knew immediately when I awoke from surgery that this new hip was at home in me. I began to walk with a comfortable rhythm, my legs were the same length, and the pain had decreased significantly. The new bone grafts went unnoticed. There was no burning or itching inside. Becky, another one of my friends from high school, surprised me with visits while I was in the hospital. She even surprised me by bringing another friend, Barbie, who was in town for a seminar, for a brief visit. We giggled and talked until we were hoarse. Margaret, also a high school friend, called and wrote letters to encourage me throughout recovery. The beauty of my high school friends is that we have remained close for over forty years now. Close friends are more precious than gold or silver. I am grateful to them for their love, devotion and honesty. We have been there for each other in joy and in sorrow. We have been honest with each another when needed even to the point of risking losing the friendship. The quality of our friendship would not be a friendship without honesty.

Dolph was moved by the devotion our group had maintained over the years. He told Becky she had been a special angel sent by God to be with me every day while I was in the hospital. Her response was: "What a sweet comment! I do not consider myself an angel sent by God, but I do believe He can prompt us to do His will. I do remember having feelings of needing to be there. I did not really try to analyze the feelings; I just knew I needed to be at the hospital. God is so good and faithful. He knows our innermost needs, even before we do. Some forty-three years ago, God 'organized' a group of girls together in high school. We did not know it then, but a lifelong friendship was forged. I praise God and give Him the Glory for those friendships."

I decided not to return to work in 2003 in order to give myself time to heal completely. Since I believed stress had been a major factor in the prolonged and unsatisfactory recovery period of the two previous hip revisions, I wanted to minimize any stress during this period of recovery. I spent extra time in rehabilitation, exercising to rebuild the muscles. It took two years to gain strength in the muscles and to be able to throw away my cane. Three surgeries in a year-and-a-half had traumatized the muscles and the sciatic nerve in ways that made me question if they were ever going to return to normal. They ached, cramped and burned from over-fatigue. Being awakened in the night to walk out a severe leg cramp was common.

The muscles were too weak to support me without the continued support of a cane.

After a series of Botox shots to the cramping muscles, many trips to the health food store for joint support supplements and continued prayers for complete healing, the muscle spasms ceased and the pain lessened. Then, miraculously, strength returned and the pain almost disappeared. Tears rolled down my face as I embraced the answer to prayer after such a long wait! Two years after the third revision, I was finally able to throw away my cane. The thrill of being able to carry my own tray again at the local cafeteria was beyond words. I was almost giddy in the cafeteria and no one knew why. Carrying my own tray was a symbol to me that my independence was back; the chapter of my struggles with hip surgeries was over. How strange our lives are as we go about living each day. We have so much to share with others, and we determine either it is not the right time to do so or that no one else would want to know. Everyone in that cafeteria had their own story to tell, but none of us knew what those stories were.

A home exercise program required me to begin walking on my treadmill and to make a major change to my diet to increase my energy. I was beginning to feel myself again. After a long five years of pain, limited range of motion, loss of my independence, the death of my mother, repeated disappointments and loss of faith, I emerged renewed.

I was reminded of the Bible verse from Isaiah 40:29 and 31: "He gives power to the faint, and to him who has no might He increases their strength. But they that wait upon the LORD shall renew their strength, they shall mount up with wings as eagles, they shall run and not be weary, and they shall walk and not faint" (RSV).

I am also reminded of a story about the eagle's journey as it renews itself. When the eagle finds that it has grown weak and can no longer perform at peak levels, it goes into a cave, grinds its talons and beak down to the nub, and plucks all of its feathers out. It is said that one can then hear the eagle crying throughout the canyons. The eagle remains in the dark cave without food until the talons, beak and feathers grow back. The eagle emerges renewed. While I did not choose the pain over the last five years, I do feel that I was called into the renewing of my body, mind, emotions and soul. The healing process requires waiting and walking into and through the pain before transformation occurs. Each of the stories of my life bears witness to this as the pathway that life presented. I had spent much energy running from the obvious and running into brick walls emotionally and physically. Waiting is an active word. It includes preparing, not just sitting passively. It includes having an expectation that something will occur. It includes facing the pain and having the courage to face what is found there. It involves being one with one's self. Remaining connected to the Holy Spirit is essential for guidance and renewal. Without this guidance, we lose our way in the storms of life. Acceptance of life and the path given to us is a theme not only seen in the eagle, but we also find it in *The Lord of The Rings: The Fellowship of the Ring* when Gandalf and Frodo are talking: (I paraphrase from what I remember the words to be.)

Frodo: "I wish the ring had never come to me. I wish none of this had happened."

Gandalf: "So do all who live to see such times. But that is not for them to decide. All we have to decide is what to do with the time that is given to us. There are other forces at work, Frodo, than the will of evil. Bilbo was meant to find the ring. In which case you also were meant to have it, and that is an encouraging thought."

I believe that we are all called into a journey. We may be asked to leave behind everything we have grown dependent upon. We may be asked to bear an incredible burden. We may be given a responsibility that is beyond our experience. We may be diagnosed with a chronic or incurable disease. Eventually, the strain of constantly living with whatever it is can cause one to "wish that the burden had never come upon him or her." We find this in Frodo as well as in the Old Testament prophets. Moses wanted another mission. Jonah wanted to avoid his calling. Peter and James wanted to stay on their mountaintop and avoid the work of life. Jesus accepted His mission; yet, He did not want to suffer the physical pain of the crucifixion or the emotional agony of abandonment by God His Father.

How are the Garden of Gethsemane and Jesus's cry to God to take his cup from him and Frodo's wishing that he did not have to carry the ring alike? How was my life similar? What other areas in my life had become a burden? These questions are part of my story and I believe the story of each of us.

To come to the acceptance of the life I have been given has been a major theme in my life. I have come to realize that I have fought against God almost every step of the way. In every journey I took away from God in my struggles to find relief, He found me and reached out to offer me comfort and healing. I don't know why we suffer. I just am certain that it is part of the human condition. God has been faithful to His promise that He will never forsake me. He has always been there to finish the work that He began in me.

The search for the meaning of dreams led me to enroll in a two-year intensive dream study program.

I had seen a brochure about the Haden Institute Dream Study program and thought about attending. It was not Jungian analysis; yet, much of the information taught there was Jungian. However, it was a two-year commitment with travel three times a year. That seemed too complicated for my life at that time. Several years later in one of my ladies' study groups, one of our members brought a brochure she had received in the mail and suggested that someone from the group go to learn and bring back the information to the group. Before I realized it, I volunteered! So I enrolled and a few months later I was off to North Carolina. Being in the woods of North Carolina was both healing and deeply spiritual. My husband and I had made five other visits to this same retreat center to attend photography workshops. Returning to North Carolina was like going home. The long weekend was filled with many lectures about the history of dreams, the cultural influences on dreams and the similarities and differences among all peoples. Some of the lectures included experiential learning. I remember one in particular. The instructor asked us to get comfortable, close our eyes and to listen to an instrumental song, sensing and feeling the emotions of the music. I found myself deep in my interior grieving something that was deeper than words. After the class was over, I went to the woods to reflect what had just happened to me. Slowly I could identify the grieving as a longing for the mother-baby bonding. In part the grief was a need to connect and the sadness of realizing that bonding would never be.

At the workshop, the two largest challenges for me were, firstly, writing my personal training in the understanding of dreams in my dream journal and reading it out loud to a group of strangers. And secondly, the sharing of our dreams in small group discussions. I felt naked and extremely vulnerable. Dreams have a tendency to reveal one's innermost sacred interior self. I had spent so much of my life hiding my interior out of fear of embarrassment. And there I was in the middle of what I had so carefully avoided. I began to question if I could actually face my fears and stay in the program. Shame and a sense of inadequacy seemed a weight on my shoulders that I was unable to carry. I would hear others reflect on their dreams with what I thought was such great insight, I was acutely aware that my understanding was different. The drive to know myself more deeply pushed my pursuit of dreams. Gradually, I accepted that the way I understand dreams is my path, rather than a clone of someone else's path. Once I accepted this, it freed me to embrace the dream process.

Working with my dreams led me to decide to search again for my birth father. I began having a series of repeating dreams, about exploring the unresolved shadows of my adoption. I was unable to discount the dream's importance. I accepted the urgency and decided to follow the dream message calling me to face the unknown and receive the blessings of healing the dream offered. Many years ago, on my own, I had searched and found my biological mother. However, I was unable to find any information relating to the whereabouts of my biological father.

Because of the insistency of my recent dreams, I decided to hire a private investigator to help me find my biological father. I had a handful of legal documents that she used and within three weeks she had located him. Sadly, he had passed away in 2002. He had played baseball for Texas A & M University before leaving to serve in the United States Army Air Force during WWII. He was a Staff Sergeant for the 332nd Bombardment Squadron, 94th Bombardment Group, Eighth Bomber Command. He completed twenty-five missions in the European Theater of Operations from May 14, 1943, through October 10, 1943, for which he was awarded an Air Medal with three Oak Leaf Clusters and the Distinguished Flying Cross. He returned from the war to continue farming on his family land. He was a Mason and a leader in both his community and his church. His family was one of the long-time settlers in his Texas hometown. He came from a respectable family. I had always assumed that he was irresponsible and a person who could not make a commitment. I was challenged to revise my beliefs about his character. This new information was part of the dream's healing.

The PI told me that she had found records that stated I had been placed in foster care about a month after I was born. This was the first time that I heard this piece to the puzzle of my life. I had always assumed I had lived with my biological mother and because of her situation my needs were neglected. This is not true. I was loved and well-taken care of for the seven months prior to being placed. As proof of her loving me, she had carried me to full term and suffered the pain of relinquishing her parental rights to me. I had carried anger against her, projecting that anger onto the parents who had adopted me. Those illusions I had fabricated as truth and lived by came crumbling down. I received a love from those who have cared for me in a healing way. The truth has set me free to be grateful for her gift of giving me up. Another gift found in following my dreams.

I set a date to go to my birth father's hometown and visit his gravesite. I decided to stay at a B&B in the next town over which was about ten minutes from his grave. His hometown has six-hundred-plus people, a gas station, a post office, churches, a Masonic lodge, an antique store and a water tower.

The lady, Ruby (strangely enough my adoptive mother's name is Ruby) at the B&B told me to go to talk to Mabel at the antique store to see if she could tell me anything about my biological father. With fear and trembling that my needs would be rejected, I went to visit her. There were several ladies in the store when I got there, so I looked all around waiting for some of them to leave. Several of the ladies left and just two remained. I found a photo of the class of 1941. I asked if there might be a photograph of the class of 1940 (the graduating class of my birth father) anywhere in the stack. Mabel asked me if there was someone that I was looking for; I said yes, and I gave her his name. She asked why. I was unsure if I should answer her directly. My mind was racing with reasons why not to answer her truthfully. Before I knew it the words came tumbling out and I replied that my answer was awkward to describe but that I was his daughter who had been given up for adoption. Mabel got a blank look on her face and said that did not make any sense. She was having a difficult time processing it. I explained it several times again. The other lady who was still in the store said: "Mabel, what the lady is saying is that he had an affair!" "OH!" Mabel said. She now understood. She agreed that his wife should never know. She knew of another, Betty Jean, who was in the class of 1940 and who would have pictures. So Mabel called her and she agreed to see me.

I went to visit Betty Jean and we talked for four hours about growing up together in their hometown and her friendship with my biological father. She had elementary class pictures, tenth year and fortieth year high school reunion pictures. She scanned them and sent me home with some pictures. She was not living in their hometown at the time of my conception. That piece remains a mystery. She said that she would find out more and let me know.

I returned to my biological father's grave multiple times to sit and to say what I felt I needed to say. I had taken Tyler roses (a dozen to represent the relationship between my birth mother and him and a dozen from me), a letter I had written to him and a rock from my backyard to place on the letter to keep it from flying off in the wind. The blessings from my prayers at the grave were many but the one that stunned me most touchingly was when I said to myself without thinking first: "I love the life that your genes have given to me." I was amazed that I was able to say: "I love the life that I have been given, even with all that there is." My life's journey has brought many hardships and there have been deep resentments for those experiences. The beauty of these words is a healing balm to my soul. My heart felt truly grateful. Had I not followed the dream, I would have missed out on this most profound gift.

I did not want to leave his gravesite. I felt connected to him and blessed by the entire process. I had found a part of myself that defined my life with dignity and honor. I had built the illusion that I was less than honorable and steeped with shame. I was now certain I could hold on to the honor that I have as my family lineage.

After I got home, I scanned the already poorly scanned and copied pictures of my biological father. I was captivated by his looks and found a sense of deep love for this man that I never knew. This love was similar to the love of a bride. I was very uncomfortable with these feelings for a father figure. I believe that all desire is ultimately a desire for God and the answer to my confusing feelings would be found in Him. I asked God what this love could tell me about my relationship to Him as His bride. Many scriptures in both the Old and New Testament came to mind referring to us as being the Bride of Christ. This insight led to a new understanding of God's character and our relationship as that of "Beloved." I had only known Jesus as Beloved and God as intervenor, creator, protector and father figure. But Beloved had never been a term that I had used for God. But yes, this is true. God is beloved and the beloved bridegroom. Another illusion broken by the truth and a blessing that I would never have received had I not followed my dreams.

My dreams keep calling me to go to my parents' gravesite and talk to them. I followed the dream's leading and, taking roses, went to my parents' grave. I told them that I had found my birth father and thanked them for adopting me. I apologized for being so rebellious and turning away from them. I thanked them for loving me in spite of my rebellion. I told them that I am so grateful for the opportunities that they offered and the instruction they provided as parents. An enormous wave of gratitude came over me as I thanked them. Gratitude is a gift of grace and my heart just sat at the gravesite and absorbed as much of it as I could contain.

The family plot has several family members. I next turned to my grandparents and thanked them for all that they gave to me in my development. I finally went to my uncle's (a lawyer and judge) grave and thanked him for signing the adoption papers, which made my adoption legal.

For the last stop on my journey, I went to my birth mother's grave bringing yellow roses with red tips. The red was to symbolize the sacrifices she made in carrying me to full-term and then giving me up for adoption. I thanked her for my life and the burden she had carried on my behalf. I told her I was in a better place from the time I last visited her. I was able to tell her that I was no longer angry with her because she had died before I could talk to her. I did regret the fact that I would never know her story with my birth father. Words slipped out of my mouth and I said to my birth mother: "I love the you that is part of me. I love the me that you represent in my life." I did not know that I felt that way until the words rolled out. I was deeply moved in knowing that I love her. I also told her I had found my birth father and all the details that I knew about him. Leaving her grave was a moment of celebration and a completion of a circle of events that shaped my destiny. I know that I was given dignity and honor both through my biological lineage and from the parents who adopted me. I was given a deep desire to seek God and grace to live a life worthy of being given the gift of life. Had I not followed my dreams, I would have missed all of these blessings.

Chapter 17

A Grateful Spirit

*Gratitude is not only the greatest of virtues
but the parent of all others.*

—MARCUS TULLIUS CICERO

Life was running rather smoothly. I thought my body was indefatigable now that my hip was healed. I forgot that I had aged considerably. It seemed now that my life had calmed down, my body stopped pushing to hold together under all its stresses. Once I stopped pushing, my body fell apart in a different way. In 2005, I started to have chest pressure and difficulty breathing. I had a difficult time picking up my legs to walk. I felt heavy and was exhausted all the time. I went to the doctor and discovered that I had developed high blood pressure. After running some blood tests, he discovered that my cholesterol was high and he put me on a diet. He prescribed exercise to increase the blood flow and increase nutrition to the brain. I had not been able to exercise for the previous five years due to the pain in my hip. Now I could. With the increased exercise, I began to experience darting pains that moved from one place to another without any pattern. This new type of pain surprised me. I was tired of hurting and I had hoped to be rid of it for a while. My doctor sent me to a rheumatology specialist who diagnosed my body pain as arthritis. Medicines for blood pressure, high cholesterol and arthritis were prescribed. I had to get a bigger pillbox!

More changes. I was tired of changes. I discovered that for self-preservation, I had become set in my ways and I did not want to change. My life had been out of my control for so many years; I had only recently been able to restructure my life with some sense of predictability and independence. I wanted to have quality in my life, so I began the recommended program of medications, diet and exercise. At the next visit to the doctor, he discovered that I had a mass in my abdomen. When the doctor told me the diagnosis, I felt sick to my stomach. I asked the doctor what it might be and he said that he suspected a reoccurrence of endometriosis from many years ago; he would not know until a sonogram was performed. It took great effort to keep from focusing on the worst possible scenario or crying in the office. All the way home, I felt so alone in my fears. Some things just do not seem to quit.

I had many questions and fears emerge in the time between being told there was a problem and not knowing what to call it.

I thought I was going to be able to handle my fears just in my own prayer time. But the Sunday before the Monday I was to receive the prognosis from the blood work and the sonogram, I realized I was unable to find peace. I had attempted to pray my fears away, I had given my fears to Jesus hundreds of times, and then the fears would jump back into my consciousness. I had a mass in my pelvic region, and I was *scared* beyond words.

Waiting to go to the doctor for the results tested my pride, my faith and my ability to accept life. It tested my capacity to reach out to others. It shook my very foundation all over again. I was reminded that life is still an ongoing journey. There are many calm times. There are many challenging times and there are many times, when in the depths of agony, there is the blessedness of growth. The solution to this current situation might be simple. Nevertheless, the negative kept jumping into my mind and it wandered all the way to the extreme. My body began to shake with fear. In pride, I did not choose to call any of my friends to ask for prayer. The very essence of life is not a guarantee. I realized I still had some spiritual work to do.

In an Episcopal church that I had previously attended, the minister gave, as a special blessing in the Eucharist service, a portion of the priest's host bread to any member of the congregation who had a special need. I believed this practice was a ritual all Episcopal ministers followed. I have since come to understand that is not the case. However, on this particular day, I believed the minister had special reasons why he chose to give a portion from the priest's host bread (the communion wafer used during the initial portion of the Eucharistic liturgy).

After entering the church on this day, I knelt in prayer. I surrendered my future once again to God for His will to be done. I asked for the reassurance that He would be there no matter what the outcome of the test results. I asked that the minister would be led by the Holy Spirit to give to me a special portion from the priest's host at the communion table as my way of knowing that my prayers were heard. When it was time for communion, I went forward. I was kneeling at the altar rail with my hands outstretched, and the minister placed in them a special portion from the priest's host. Peace washed over me and I was full. It was as if I heard God say I am with you *always*. From that moment, I was devoid of fear about the surgery or its outcome.

I went into surgery confident God was with me. My emotions were no longer focused on fear of dying or of having cancer. They had shifted to remaining in union with the God who loves me. The tumor turned out to be of benign substance. There were no complications from surgery and recovery was rapid.

Why was this surgery easy when it took three surgeries to fix my hip? I have no idea. God heals in His way, in His order and in His time. One of the things that I have found was that God healed me according to His priorities, not mine. I have found that He repeatedly puts spiritual healing first. Just as God's healings were operative in my transformation, it was necessary for the obstacles, which hindered me from the transformation, to be removed. What lessons did I carry with me into this crisis this time? I was given a grateful spirit. I accepted a willingness to accept. I was able to let go of pride. With God's help, I could walk into another valley, with assurance God was there to walk the path with me no matter what.

Given that the transitions of my life have been ever changing, I am certain that my golden years will not be any different. I have already begun the evaluation of the questions: "What do I want to do with the time that is left?" And "How do I want to live with quality and meaning in the future?" I have begun to downsize and give away possessions that seem to be in the way. I am surrounding myself only with things that bring me joy. If I am not using "it," it is no longer in my possession. I used to have five storage sheds of memories and now I have reduced the clutter. I am interested in many hours of quiet time. My body and energy levels are slowing down. I choose what I want to do rather than what others want me to do. I seek quality rather than quantity. I do maintain my group of close friends and I do have ways I serve in my community. I continue to offer spiritual direction and I am active in leading dream study groups. I remain enthusiastic about my photography. I attend workshops as a way of deepening my understanding of creativity and photography.

I read, exercise, get sunshine and attempt to stay on a heart-healthy diet (which is not easy for me.) I am challenged daily by the pains of arthritis. Each day I begin with prayer and a grateful attitude. It is important to me to keep an active mind, nurture my ability to be flexible and strive for a positive outlook. Staying involved will help to keep me young and live longer. Sixty-seven is a time when I need to do what I can to maintain a healthy lifestyle. I am learning that no matter what happens to my body, my quality of life is not dependent on my health. I also am learning that any illness I might incur is not my identity. The way I take care of my body will allow me to have a longer life to enjoy.

Even though I am in my senior years, I have a life of experiences to share. I also believe I still have much to learn about life and myself. I hope the quest never ends. I look forward to continued learning and continued sharing with others. My spiritual quest for the God I love continues to pull me into an even deeper relationship with Him.

> *As with any relationship, the more you get to know someone that you love, the more you want to know about him or her.*

As with any relationship, the more you get to know someone that you love, the more you want to know about him or her. My love for God is no different. I have only just begun to walk the spiritual walk. I will continue to reach deep within to search for the truth. I think that I am going to like growing older. I have gained great wisdom from life that could not have been gained through textbooks.

Moving into my senior years will continue to be an adventure for me. I am relying on these latter years to be the richest ever in my spiritual growth, with increased wisdom gained through the living of my life. The more I have learned, the more I realize I do not know much about anything. I have just begun to learn. I hunger for more of life and the gifts that are offered to me.

Looking back on a prayer that was beside my mother's bed, which I have now adopted as one of my own, I find that the words speak to the very essence of my life with my loving Creator and Healer:

> I asked for strength that I might achieve;
> I was made weak that I might obey.
> I asked for health that I might do greater things;
> I was given infirmity that I might do better things.
> I asked for riches that I might be happy;
> I was given poverty that I might be wise.
> I asked for power that I might have the praise of men;
> I was given weakness that I might feel the need of God.
> I asked for all things that I might enjoy life;
> I was given life that I might enjoy all things.
> I have nothing that I asked for but everything I hoped for.
> My prayers *are* answered.
> I am most blessed.
>
> —Anonymous

Chapter 18

PUTTING IT ALL TOGETHER

It is not in the pursuit of happiness that we find fulfillment but in the happiness of the pursuit.

—DENIS WAITLEY

Not all of my life was consumed with struggles or pain. I have had many wonderful experiences that have also brought about transformation. The sight of a breathtaking sunset or rainbow, for example, has the power to fill my soul with wonder. Wonder is healing. Nature is able to communicate life and the gift of life that we have been given. Taste, touch, smell and sight all enable me to experience life in a mystical way. I am more than flesh and blood.

As I have mentioned, our family returned to the same place every year for a vacation. We were able to take side trips into the mountains, and healing came when I was there. Yearly, I would feel renewed as I would smell the mountain air and see the strength that the mountains would express. I sensed the family was in harmony with one another. The mountains had running streams from freshly melted snow. I loved to wade in the water even though it was cold. The running streams would bring me comfort and renewal. The everyday cares of life were postponed for a month. For me, the mountains are where God lives. They appear so strong and powerful. They have a presence of having been there for a long time, and I know the next time I return, they will still remain.

Humor was healing. Laughter in relationships, but not laughing at someone else, was healing. Merriment in dancing or gatherings (I am not referring to a party that has mind-altering drugs or alcohol) brought healing. Appreciation for the arts in all forms brought healing. Appreciation was healing. Joy was healing. Developing and maintaining a joyful spirit was healing. Gratitude for everything in life was healing. Forgiveness heals across time. Wonderment restored the child within. A deep abiding faith and belief in something greater than myself helped to bring security and an awareness of who I was created to be. Time out was healing, too, for a break brought me back to my center. It was necessary for me to take a yearly vacation to a place I yearned to go. Time out also included reading a good book or meditation time. The point of the time out was to establish once again who was in control of my life and to withdraw from the demands of life and others. Spontaneous play was healing. Being creative was healing. Risking my boundaries to adventure into something I had always wanted to do but was afraid to do was healing.

It did not matter what modality was used to bring about transformation in my life. They all came from the same guiding source. I was surprised that I was given such a variety of paths. God has given me the ability to see Him in all things and in all people. He has shown me I can find Him anywhere. He has taught me the focus of my life *is* to seek Him. He has proved He is faithful in all of my circumstances and has never abandoned His love or intervention for me. He has spoken to me through every event recorded in this book.

My transformation process led me to look seriously into the physical, psychological and spiritual dimensions of my life. In the transitions my life advanced through, I moved differently on those three plains, yet they overlapped each other. Physically, I evolved from conception to seniorhood. My body has changed shape and I have experienced the aging process. My body has absorbed all the stresses as my front line of defense. The body has memory and remembers everything. The "body memory" asked for healing as well. It has worn down several times and was in need of medical intervention. Because of the body's natural ability to heal, it recovered successfully.

> *The body has memory and remembers everything.*

Psychologically, I transitioned from abandonment, insecurity, low self-esteem, worthlessness, anxiety, rage, inadequacy in handling a situation, loneliness, helplessness in the victim role, shame and mistrust to having personal boundaries, healthy self-appraisal, authority, a sense of connection, competency, a willingness to communicate and to the forgiveness of others and self.

"Father forgive them; for they know not what they do." (Luke 23:34, RSV) These are the recorded words of Jesus from the cross. I have given several examples of how forgiving someone who hurt me, because I believed that they were remorseful, brought healing in my heart. I have also given examples of how forgiving others, even though they had no remorse for their hurts, also healed me. In rage or resentfulness against another, I believe there is a powerful chemical that is released into the system. This chemical can begin to destroy the body. When I have held resentment, I have experienced headaches, digestive disorders and heart trouble, to name a few. The person responsible for the hurt generally did not experience the damaging chemical change because of his or her actions. I have observed a strange phenomenon relating to forgiveness. The phenomenon was apparent when I had been hurt by someone who would not ask for forgiveness, but I chose to forgive that person anyway. The reason to forgive is because "they do not know what they do" in the overall plan of life. It is not condoning what they did. Nor is it negating the hurtfulness of the actions. Forgiveness is bigger than that. It is related to truly believing that the person does not understand how his or her actions or words affect others, the earth, and even onward out into the universe. When forgiveness is given, there sets in motion a release of energy for both persons.

If unforgivingness continues, the other person can justify his or her stance and be unwilling to face the consequences of his or her actions. Unforgivingness then actually helps the other person to continue to hurt others and to maintain blindness to his or her hurtful actions, never reaching an awareness of what he or she did and thus having no desire to ask for forgiveness.

Another reason I chose to forgive was the honest understanding that I have hurt others by my words and deeds even though I may not have hurt others in the same way that I was hurt. To be able to realistically look into my own life and evaluate my motives, words and actions enabled me to forgive others.

I went through a period of time in which I found I could not forgive God for what I believed were cruel and unnecessary situations. I went into a depth of rage. I cursed the day I was born before I came to understand God is aware and He had a magnificent plan for my life. It was humbling to face just how little I really know about God's plan for me.

The hardest of all to forgive is myself. I could accept my forgiveness of others and my forgiveness from God, even accept that others would never forgive me. It was my forgiving myself that I found difficult. I held on to the idea that if I did not forgive myself, somehow I could retain the power to erase or change the situation. Maybe it was pride. Whatever the reason, I found it difficult to forgive myself and to accept myself as a whole human being, perfectly imperfect.

I discovered a repetitive pattern: the things that almost destroyed me were the very things that set me free. Gifts in life were showered upon me in spite of all the struggles. I had previously lived emotionally frightened that I would be destroyed by events and the words of others. The emotional structure of my life was rebuilt to sustain me in most all situations. All the challenges and all of the gifts either reinforced or awakened my yearning to search for the truth, and to be set free from the past that had kept me in bondage, and from discovering and becoming the person that I was created to be.

Spiritually, my understanding of God grew deeper, wider and with more awe for His loving presence. I have moved from my will in stubbornness or fear to surrender. Looking back over my life at the development of my faith, I discovered patterns of movement and patterns of resistance to change. Each stage provided substance for transformation to the next. The more I deliberately chose to let God direct my every thought, word and action, the more profoundly my life with Him was affected. God called me continually to recognize Him in my life and to respond.

I began as a child of faith ready to accept anything having to do with God. I believed unconditionally the faith stories. Faith was simple. I talked to God, and He answered all of my dialogues. I believed He was omnipotent. I believed He intervened in my life. I believed He would provide what I needed. God was my best friend and Father/Mother. I identified with the Bible stories. As an adopted child, I formed a belief my life was similar to the life of Moses in that I was of genetic making from one family and, for God's reasons, I was raised in another. I believed and did not need to question. My self-concept of worthlessness, shame and guilt as well as mistrust of others hindered my growth until early adulthood. My body concept, the overbearing limp, the pain and the social stigma related to having dyslexia, reinforced my negative self-image. The crisis of fearing that the tumor I had was going to kill me was the impetus that sparked my growth to the next level of spiritual development.

With the revelation of the Light of Christ, I moved into service, knowledge and steadfastness in the witness to God as seen in Jesus Christ. I was busily serving in the church and verbally witnessing to the truth as it had been revealed to me. I was almost too heavenly to be of any use on earth. I had a profound sense that I was loved and called to be a disciple. However, I was timid about allowing God to have His way with my emotions. I kept finding excuses to hold on to the negative self-esteem. It took alcoholism to shake me loose from holding so tightly to the past.

Recovering from alcoholism sent me into the depths of this person was who was created in the image of God. Accepting my heritage as a child of God was a gift from God Himself. I felt the presence of the Holy Spirit leading me into self-discovery in a way that was painful. Had I known beforehand that I would be put in the furnace to burn away the chaff, I might not have gone.

When physical pain returned into my life, I turned and ran from the gift of intimate friendship that God was offering. I began to question why He was allowing me to hurt. I lost the patience of my youth to endure. I found myself in a spiritual crisis like no other time in my life. I questioned the omnipotent power of God. I questioned if God answers prayers for some and not others.

Self-realization can be scary and is very painful. I felt the burden of hurting so many people. I was asked to see clearly my responsibility for my actions. It was difficult to separate the spiritual healing in this phase from the psychological. God was offering me wholeness and not dividing me into specific sections. As the psychological side of me was in the process of healing, so was the spiritual and vice versa. A loving hand guided me in word and in deeds. In spite of all my own efforts, God brought me through the furnace to the side of illumination. I was beginning to embrace my humanity. I was beginning to forgive myself for things I had done and things I had left undone that God had given to me to do. I began to see the talents I had been given that I had wasted. I was not the one who orchestrated the events or insights that brought me safely to the next level of understanding. I was aware God was calling me, and all I had to do was respond to His leading. I began to relinquish more of my life and my will in obedience to God. The more I gave to Him, the more He blessed me with Himself.

Once illuminated, I was surprised to discover that there is so much more. The God I had known was outgrowing my limited understanding of Him. He showered me with dreams and symbols as teaching tools. I began to realize I really knew nothing at all about God. I had witnessed the Light of Christ, the ongoing power of the Holy Spirit and the assurance that God was the same God throughout all history, but I knew nothing really. My desire to engage in an intimate relationship with God became a hunger I could not satisfy. I began classes in spiritual direction; I immersed myself in more Bible study, and joined a group that was exploring spirituality. I was filled with the desire to disconnect from the ties and attachments of this world. My lifestyle changed to include more solitude and less clutter. I was learning rapidly that God is in all but that even the "all" does not define God. The closer I moved to God, the more He revealed to me and the more I realized how little I really knew.

Psychologically, I was called to higher level of letting go of the ties that had kept me locked into the past. I spent much time trying to initiate the answers. I wore myself out striving to make my life less painful. Seeking therapy again opened the doors for psychological and spiritual transformation. I call that period of growth a "dark night of my soul" because I felt withered and alone. I searched but did not find. I grieved but still felt that I was losing. I felt alone and thought that God had abandoned me. I was being called to relinquish something in my identity. Giving it up did not mean losing although it felt like it at the time. It did mean to detach from whatever was preventing me from walking humbly and obediently with God. He was providing all the open doors for me to walk through. He was holding the candle in the darkness. I was over in the corner complaining about my pain and that no one cared about me. Oh, how wonderful and gracious God is. He

> *Giving it up did not mean losing although it felt like it at the time.*

faithfully held on to me. He did not abandon me, even though I turned and ran. The realization that He has always been with me no matter where I went or how I got there brought me to my knees, and not just literally.

Spiritually, I came to see a loving guide and friend. I do not have any answers for why I was allowed to hurt for so long, or why He seems to answer some prayers and why He waits to answer others. I do not yet even have a way of describing God. He remains to be seen through a mist and only experienced as an elusive presence. Spiritual growth for me has only begun. I do not expect that I will arrive at completion in this lifetime. But, oh, the journey is invigorating.

Chapter 19

STORIES FROM THE OTHER CHAIR

*Making a broken life into a whole story is the
most powerful act of healing possible.*

—ELIZABETH J. ANDREW

My professional career as a psychotherapist and spiritual director has brought many challenges and rewards. I have heard stories that would break my heart and stories that bring celebration. In this chapter, I will give several examples from the other chair in my therapy room to further show how difficult it is not only to begin but also to continue the lifetime search for wholeness. When the pain in our life becomes too intense, it is common to seek advice, guidance or counseling. When the pain has passed, it is easy to forget and return to old habits. Life is a series of forward, backward, sidestepping and denial. Freedom is in truth and the pursuit of it.

There are several reasons why people come to therapy: to get an immediate situation resolved and to prevent the situation from occurring again; to explore other issues that might be interfering with the journey toward wholeness; and to seek God's direction. Only a few persons stay in therapy or spiritual direction until they reach a sense of completion. Life is ongoing and so is the healing process.

I have found that all people who have shared their stories with me are searching for answers to such questions as: Who am I? Why am I here? Why is this happening to me? Where do I go from here? How do I cope? How can we get along together? I would like to share a few stories with you now, as told to me by others, as examples of our human condition.

No Way. I Am Not Changing.

Change is hard. It needs to come from a deep commitment to consider all aspects of one's life, something that many people have a tough time doing.

Will's Story

Will came to my office because he was suffering with anxiety. He shared with me his story about his family of origin and how his father was rather violent. As he described his intense hatred for his father, his face became red and his breathing increased. He raged as he blamed his father for all of his life problems. He blamed his father for the way he was coping with life now. He was supersensitive and very self-absorbed. As a defense against feeling out of control, he had learned to manipulate others to get what he wanted. He shared that he knew how to move into someone's emotions and attack him or her there. He knew he had power over them at that point. If that did not work, then he would become physically violent. He was unwilling to relinquish one form of power to learn another. His concept of power did not include compromise, debate, the possibility of not getting what he wanted or personal responsibility. We discussed why he was in therapy and he came to the decision that, if he had to change his manipulative behaviors in any way to reduce his anxiety, he would not change. At that point in his life, he was not willing to go through the uncertainty and chaos necessary to resolve the issues, nor was he willing to take responsibility for his own life's choices. He chose to keep his rage and his cruel manipulation, even if it cost him a high level of anxiety. He did not return to therapy.

ANN'S STORY

Ann came to talk with me because she was not able to adjust to a new medical diagnosis. She spent much of the initial session giving examples about how her body was giving way. She had been for several consultations to seek a different diagnosis. It is a normal reaction to resist a lifestyle-altering diagnosis. There is usually a period of denial, of anger or resistance, of seeking many other opinions, of bargaining with something greater than oneself, of depression and then, hopefully, of learning to live with the situation. Each session, we were processing the same issue: she did not want to be sick and she was just plain angry. The angrier she got, the sicker she got. Transferring her to a medical doctor for an antidepressant was her best solution. Therapy could not make the external situation go away, and that was her goal for coming.

Hank's Story

Hank came to my office because of prescription abuse. He just wanted to stop his drug pattern of addiction. We discussed his history of drug abuse. We discussed drug relapse prevention, which would require changes that would be permanent. He began to do the work required. He began to identify patterns of emotions and responses. He began to risk taking responsibility for his thoughts, feelings and beliefs. As we began to delve into his caretaking role and how that defined his identity, he began to resist changing. As reported by a family member, one afternoon after a difficult session, Hank went home, curled into a fetal position on the floor in the corner of his bedroom and withdrew into a nap. At the next session, he returned to therapy and announced that he would not change. He was not going to do any more work. For, if he did change, he would no longer know who he was. Moving through the pain was too difficult for him at that time in his life. He has since returned to his pattern of substance abuse.

Betty's Story

Betty came to my office because she wanted help from me in filing for disability with the Social Security Administration. She had already been told by several doctors that she was too young to just give up on her life without learning new coping skills. She had a panic disorder, which interfered with her ability to keep a steady job. Whenever she was overcome with panic, she was unable to function. She had never learned coping skills that would help to reduce the intensity of her attacks. She was given the option to learn new skills and then to evaluate her need for SSDI assistance. She refused. Her goal was to remain in the role of "sick." She was getting her needs met by being ill. I never saw her again. Some people do not get well because they want the benefits that they perceive to be gained from being ill.

Completing the Task

The journey is never ending. The goal is to reach a point when we know how to travel.

Anthony and Lucy's Story

I had a father and his daughter come into therapy. He brought her in because she had announced to him that she had chosen the lesbian lifestyle. She stated that it had been a difficult and lonely journey into the darkest corners of her heart, but that she had come to the awareness that this was who she was. He became irate because his wish for his daughter was not her choice. He screamed at me because I could not "fix" her and ran out of the room, never to return. His daughter continued to commit to therapy, and with hard work, she developed a sense of honor and respect for herself that she had never had. She retired from therapy feeling whole. She had been restored to herself through forgiveness and true self-acceptance.

PETE'S STORY

I visited Pete who had just been brought into the hospital because of third-degree burns to his hands. He was in excruciating pain and frightened not only about being able to keep his hands but also about what the future would hold for him. His hands were bandaged, and he had been given a heavy dose of medication. The medication was not reducing the pain. After he was able to let go of his macho facade and truthfully describe his fears and his vulnerability, his pain level reduced. He was able to sleep. I am convinced that his willingness to talk about his fears assisted his body in moving toward recovery. He actually recovered the full use of his hands; he had no scarring.

CAROL'S STORY

As the therapist on a hospice team, I walked with a very special woman, Carol, through her journey into death. On one particular day that I visited her, she was having a crisis about the meaning of her life and her death. Much of her suffering was related to an inability to engage the deepest questions of life. She was essentially lonely because no one was there with whom to share her journey. She was living in her daughter's home but did not want to upset her daughter by talking about death. She felt terror as she contemplated going through "the valley of the shadow of death" alone. I listened while she remembered her life and the events of special meaning. I listened as she shared business that was not yet finished. I listened as she defined her faith in a way that allowed questions.

After our visit, I went to a park near her home. I picked up leaves from an oak tree and maple tree. I picked up acorns as well. Fall had already come and the leaves were changing colors. The next day I took my collection to her home. We talked about the cycle of life from birth (the acorn) through the dying process (the turning leaves) and then on to death (the very dried, dark brown leaves.) The acorn also symbolized that it had to separate from the life of the tree before it could seed into the ground and produce new life. She was blessed with the comfort that she needed to face her fears.

Several months later, as she was in the last few hours of her life, she told me that she was convinced we all get to have an escort into death. She told me that she had asked to be mine and that she would be back for me. She was able to face her fears in death and find peace.

Amanda and Justin's Story

Amanda came to my office because she was suffering with a chronic debilitating disease. She easily fatigued all the time. Justin, her husband, was having difficulty adjusting to the lifestyle changes that she needed to make. She had been a faithful serving wife. Now he resented that he had to sometimes put his free time aside to assist her. He began to express his resentment through aggressive and abusive behaviors.

When she came into my office, she was separated, bruised and confused. Both she and her husband eventually were able to face their concepts of the masculine and feminine roles and admit to each other their hopes for the relationship and their fears for the future. They were able to risk being vulnerable with one another, which literally set them free to embrace a meaningful relationship. Reaching that level of communication was a process. Justin stopped coming for a time but returned because he loved her more than he loved his need to be aggressive against her.

Brad's Story

Brad, a Native American, came to therapy because of his alcoholism and aggressive behavior. He grew up on a reservation. He and the other members had been converted to the Baptist faith. He had lost connection with his Indian roots. He had been through several rehab centers and was again back in the cycle of drinking. We focused on his realigning himself with his roots. I listened to his story about his life on the reservation. I listened to his beliefs and his grief in losing what had been passed down through many generations. Spirituality is not a set of beliefs; it is life itself. One benefit that had been passed down to him was that he was to remain stoic. Yet, he was acting out his confusion in inappropriate ways. He had lost a sense of pride for himself and for his heritage.

The more we talked about his roots, the more he was able to connect. We found a rehab center that incorporated Native American traditions into his healing modality. I discharged him from my care, transferring him on to continue exploring his roots. No matter which culture is ours, there is a rich history that, when it is lost or devalued, causes a loss of identity. That young man had the courage both to face his nightmares and to reach out again to seek answers.

ALBERT'S STORY

One of the most profound transformations that I witnessed was when I walked with Albert, a middle-aged man, who had just lost his father, his business, his marriage and his only brother. He was bordering on depression. To maintain his ability to work, he minimized the intensity of his situation. He had the courage to face the grief of losing his father and his brother. He was able to accept his part in the destruction of his marriage while also acknowledging his wife's responsibility. He was able to face and resolve the loss of his business and the identity he associated with his losses.

Therapy was not the only way he grew. He also sought spiritual direction. He read many books relating to healing and talked with other men about the deeper meanings of life. His goal was to find peace and wholeness. It has taken him ten years to find the peace within that he was seeking. He has begun to enjoy the search for wholeness and is committed to spending the rest of his life in pursuit of that goal.

Chapter 20

IT IS YOUR TURN

Life is of roadblocks, dead ends, hills, change, misery and crises.
But life is also full of joy, gladness, wonder, love and awe.
The difference? My reaction and my focus.

– A CLIENT

A life story is ever evolving. New insights are gained when events are connected, as I call it—connecting the dots, that hadn't previously been paired. Wisdom (the ability to think and act using knowledge, experience and insight) never ends for growth continues as reflection about life naturally unfolds. We are always walking toward the light of illumination.

In the writing of this manuscript, I was surprised to have been blessed in new and different ways. New insights came together that I had not previously considered. For example, as I was discussing my journey with Dyslexia as written in this manuscript with Michael, the grandson of my sister-in-law. Without knowing the significance of the question, he asked me if the type of Dyslexia I had was that I saw all letters and numbers backwards or transposed all or just some. He also asked if I saw the letters clearly some of the time. No one had ever asked me that question that way before. After thinking about his question, I responded, some of the time. He responded, "That must have been confusing for you." My memories, thoughts and emotions went high speed to the past. Life events seemed to fall like dominos. I understood a core reason as to how my lack of trusting my intuition or decision-making process led to a lack of self-confidence, of self trust was born I began to trust my own judgment. I doubted my capacity to make an accurate decision.

I remember a time when the family was picnicking near a stream in Colorado. Mother told me to stay close and not to adventure to the other side of the stream. Curiosity and adventure over powered mother's warning. On the other side of the stream, I found many things to see. I heard mother calling so I hurriedly took a shortcut back. However, I ended up in a trail of thorns. There was no way out but to go on through the pricks and sticks to reach the bank before I could return to the other side. OUCH! Into my foot went a thorn. I had a difficult time getting the long thorn out of my barefoot standing on the other leg. If I fell I would end up on the ground in more thorns. Returning to the picnic area, I did not tell mother I had been wounded. Hiding under the veil of silence protected me from exposure. This was a common theme in my life. Hiding under the veil of silence in order to protect myself. Within a few days the foot became infected. I began to limp to avoid the pain. I could no longer hide my actions. Confession, openly revealing my situation, was the only to bring healing. A trip to the doctor, medication and I was on my way to healing. I mention this memory because it is symbolic of a significant life pattern. Hiding always led to pain and then the issue festered into an even larger wound. The more I denied the reality of my situation, the more ill I became. The only way to heal was to face my life squarely and admit it not only to myself but also to others. Hiding lead me to withdraw and live isolated. Healing was possible only when I began to reach out to others for help. There have been many other thorns I have had to walk on in this life. *Walking On Thorns* is a story about these thorns and the healing journey through pain. Each thorn has taught me a lesson about courage, persistence, and facing the truth.

When I reread my manuscript, I discovered that I had not put the two rape experiences together or questioned what their effect on my marriage had been. I found it interesting that just prior to my marriage was date rape, and just prior to the marriage ending was, again, rape. My marriage was sandwiched in between the two rape experiences, so to speak. It became clear that because I had not processed the date rape, my ability to mature into a healthy trusting remains relationship in my marriage was hindered. The effects of the date rape were far more reaching than I had actually imagined.

Another example that came to mind was realizing that finding the fire on our Christmas tree just as the first spark ignited actually saved my family's lives. They had time to crawl out and avoid the smoke inhalation. I had been so focused on failing to get under the tree to unplug the lights that I lost sight of the most important gift: I had been led to the Christmas tree just in time to see the spark and save their lives.

I had also never considered the similarities between the need for a second surgery right after my hysterectomy and the need to have a second surgery almost immediately following the first hip revision. Both brought up feelings of disbelief, disappointment, anger and added hardship on my body. My body has been through so much hardship. I saw a new opportunity to be grateful for this body I have been given. I have an opportunity to admit how strong my body remains it is strong in spite of how weak I have always felt it was. Not weak in the sense I cannot lift anything heavy but in the sense it has been able to weather so many surgeries and continue to bounce back. Such information and insight bring wholeness to one's story. Being able to see my life in these new ways seemed to bring form. Order was created out of chaos and I was blessed with new understanding.

I believe that each of us has a story to tell. It can be told from many different angles and at different times in one's life. It can be told about one event or about as many events as needed to communicate the point. It can be told in chronological order or very much out of order. It can be written from a physical, emotional, and/or spiritual perspective. My story was written from all three perspectives. Your story can be written from the account of what is called a genogram, or a family tree, which places the story in patterns of beliefs and values that have been passed down from one person to another and from one generation to the next. Your story can be in journal format or in the format of a memoir, a poem, a short story or a mystery novel. It can be autobiographical or truth disguised as fiction. The finished product can be stored under your bed or in a safety deposit box. It can be shared with a friend, with family or with a therapist. It can be burned or buried. The process and the insights gained will remain with you forever. Your story is not limited to writing. It can be sung, painted, sculpted or danced. Any imaginable creative expression will allow your story to be told. I encourage you to put your life in a form for you to see and possibly to be shared with others. The healing power of this exercise is beyond your wildest dreams.

It is very important to ensure that you are safe when you write. Writing tends to bring up many memories. Writing can help you to heal, but I suggest that you proceed slowly and cautiously. If you ever feel you are at risk, for example, of losing control or acting on dangerous thoughts, you should consult a qualified professional therapist. If you are already in therapy, I suggest that you talk to your therapist about and before starting this project. I want to make it very clear here, that writing your story alone is not recommended for individuals who are vulnerable to a psychotic process, to severe depression or who have experienced severe traumas in the past. Trained professionals should be available for those individuals.

In the last entry of Reflections from Jeanne's Journey, I offer you a possible outline for writing your story.

Living by example is a form of telling your story. Is the life that you are living the one that you desire others to know? To live by example calls one to be whom and what he or she believes. It requires that one has examined one's motives, one's intent, one's values, one's behaviors and one's words; really, to evaluate everything. An unexamined life is a barren wasteland. There is much to be discovered when one risks looking within.

We are not able to function effectively in the present without knowledge of who we have been in the past.

Our life is impossible without memory. We are not able to function effectively in the present without knowledge of who we have been in the past. The past is the womb of the future and at each moment, the present is born. The narrative of your life story is the arena in which God, through whatever means deemed necessary, acts to re-create you. I do not believe our spiritual life can deepen fully outside of an awareness of our personal history.

This book has been about my life as an ongoing process through the painful valleys and beyond. There had to be a death before there could be a birth. There had to be a birth before there was a death. Order came from chaos. The chaos was actually necessary so that order could be formed. Nothing is considered hidden until it is known. I have become transformed as I have risked looking at situations and persisting until I embraced the rewards. I had the opportunity to revisit some of my unfinished business at later developmental stages so that my wholeness could be more complete. My life story is always a work of art in progress. As I progressed along life's journey, I continued to see miracles that opened my eyes to the wonder of who I am.

By what truths do we live? By what truths do we understand who we are? Where do we invest our energies during this brief time called life? Are we living the life that we chose, or are we living someone else's life choices for them? By what point of reference do we make our decisions? How are you allowing your life to unfold? The self stands at the core of being. It is the carrier of what the soul intends. This calling to peace in the inner self will not make our life easy or free of suffering nor will it win the praises of our friends or community, but it will fill our life with meaning, purpose and a general sense of the rightness of our life's path.

Storytelling has always been at the heart of being human. I believe we have the need to pass along our traditions and our heritage. We need to humbly confess our shortcomings and failings. We need to find healing of present or past wounds. We need to be able to bring hope to a suffering world. We need to connect with a larger community. Peace begins within before it can be offered without.

As a witness to another's story, I may discover that someone else has a problem similar to mine, and as I hear it or read it in another person's words, I may gain new insights into my own dilemma. Sometime, as I hear or read an individual explore possible resolutions to his or her problem, my own inner teacher is awakened.

At the very least, knowing that someone else has a problem like mine gives me a sense of not being crazy or alone.

Because our stories make us vulnerable to others who may want to fix us or exploit us, or dismiss us or ignore us, we have learned to tell guardedly or not at all. Instead of telling our story, we talk about our opinions, ideas and beliefs rather than about our lives. We discount our struggles as though they are weaknesses to hide. I am convinced that neighbors, coworkers and even family members can live side by side for years, maybe even a lifetime, without learning much about the others' lives. As a result, I believe that we lose something of great value. For in truly seeing another person, we must seek to understand his or her situation and then we are able to have a fuller understanding of ourselves.

All the tools that you need to write your story are within you. You were a witness to the events. You experienced them. You saw them happen. You felt them in your body. You have a depth of emotions that go along with the events. The words are waiting for expression.

My prayer for you, the reader, is that you will be blessed in the telling of your life's story. "Lord, help others to remember where they have been and how You have walked the journey of life by their side. Lord, bring forth the essence of the lives of your people so that their lives and their memories will be a testimony to Your redeeming quality. Amen."

I now invite you to begin the journey of writing your own unique story and of finding the mystery and blessings therein.

Reflections from Jeanne's Journey

During my journey, I faced many situations and asked many questions. To help you with your journey, I revisit those questions in this section of the book. The topics and questions are placed in the order in which the issues appear in the text.

The Forces That Shape You

To know yourself you need to have an understanding of the forces that shaped you. Your parents, siblings and family culture will have undoubtedly contributed to your development. Here are a few simple questions designed to help you consider these influences: what they were, how they shaped you and how you have, or have not, come to terms with them.

What role(s) did you play in your family? (For example: caregiver, peacemaker, rebel, clown, dutiful child, odd man out, etc.)

Have you repeated these roles in other relationships? _____
_____

How have you been able to escape these roles? _____
_____
_____

How did you see your mother as a child?

How do you see your mother now?

How did you see your father as a child?

How do you see your father now?

How did you see your siblings as a child?

How do you see them now? _____
_____
_____

How did you see yourself as a child? _____
_____
_____

How did you see yourself as a teenager? _____
_____
_____

How did you see yourself as a young adult? _____
_____
_____

What physical dispositions (e.g., food allergies, specific disease risks) did you get from:

    a) biological mother   b) biological father

What psychological dispositions (e.g. worry, depression, inattention) did you get from:

    a) mother   b) father   c) other caregivers

Reflections from Jeanne's Journey
Self-Definition

Our self-definition comes from not who we are but what we can do and how well we're doing it. Personal evolution helps move you to make that transition from seeing yourself as a set of skills to viewing yourself as a whole person with meaning beyond a set of abilities. Skills, and lack thereof, are often a function of forces over which we have no control, like genetics. But, naturally, I interpreted that to mean there was something wrong with me. The more we believe that we are defined by our performance, the more pressure there is to succeed. The more there is of not doing well in a task the more it is a reflection of us.

QUESTIONS:

How do you judge how good you are at a certain skill? _____

_____

_____

_____

Do you ever feel that you are just not good enough? _____

_____

How do you evaluate yourself as a person?

How do you evaluate others?

Reflections from Jeanne's Journey
Social Comparison

As we get older, we realize that for the most part, what other people think of us doesn't materially matter, unless they are integrated into our lives: for example, family members or managers with some authority over us. But there seems to be an innate sense that compels us to compare ourselves to others. There's no question that some people are more obsessed with status than others, but the need to know where we are in the pecking order seems to be hardwired into the human brain. I suspect that it is one of those aspects of the primal brain that, to some extent, has outlived its usefulness. Primitive man was tribal and every member was dependent on the group. Being low down on the food chain was a serious threat to survival. For primitive man, status meant safety. This has led us today to still be overly concerned about what other people think about us. We still naturally compare ourselves and it isn't difficult to feel we come up short. And when we come up short, we blame ourselves. Connection is important because at one point in our existence it was the key to survival.

The famous psychologist Albert Ellis, father of Rational-Emotive therapy, said that the most common thinking error is to want or expect everyone to love you. As he pointed out, this often leads to codependency in an effort to get love and depression when it's not forthcoming. Where does this need come from? Is it part of the primal brain's need for security that comes from acceptance and belonging?

Questions:

How much influence do other people's opinions have on you? _____

_____

How do you react to criticism? _____

_____

_____

How do people form opinions? _____

_____

_____

How much effort do you make to get appreciation and positive attention from others? _____

_____

_____

What do others think of you? _____

_____

_____

Reflections from Jeanne's Journey
Shame, disgrace and humiliation

There's that status "where am I in the pecking order" notion again. Shame, disgrace and humiliation have a social element to them; it's not just that you feel inadequate or guilty but you assume or know that others are belittling you. Shame can be crippling and make one want to withdraw in every possible way. Shame, not depression, is the more common underlying emotion driving suicide. Because of social comparison, our need to belong can amplify our shame and make us feel that hopeless and helpless.

QUESTIONS:

Have you ever felt shame? _____

_____

How did you feel? _____

_____

_____

_____

_____

How did you overcome it? _____

_____
_____
_____
_____
_____

Are you judgmental of others? _____

_____

What would you say to others who felt shame? _____

_____
_____
_____
_____
_____

Reflections from Jeanne's Journey
Performance Anxiety

The smooth performance of almost any task, especially a motor task, is best done implicitly, (i.e., without conscious thought). Consciousness interrupts performance. Go to an amateur theatrical production and you can watch local accountants, lawyers and others who have sensibly kept their daytime jobs, try to act. Some are good but many seem to be watching themselves act, consciously prompting their own performance. Watch a professional and there's none of that; he or she is simply in the role, implicitly in character.

When you are learning a task, (e.g., driving), behavior is explicit in that you have to consciously attend to every movement. Over time and with practice, the behavior doesn't need conscious attention and it becomes implicit. Practice might not make perfect, but practice makes implicit. I was to learn that my evolution had to be painfully and self-consciously explicit before it became implicit. Which means that the journey to self-actualization can be full of doubt and anxiety.

Questions:

Do you suffer from performance anxiety? _____

_____

What skills or behaviors are associated with anxiety for you? _____

_____

_____

_____

_____

_____

How do you manage any anxiety you have before performing a task?

_____

_____

_____

_____

_____

Reflections from Jeanne's Journey
Handling Emotions

Learning about emotions and how to handle them is a critical part of life and that training begins the moment we come in to this world, if not before. One of the most critical parenting skills is to teach children about emotions: what they are, why we have them, and more importantly, how to think about them, talk about them and manage them. But how many parents even recognize this, let alone know how to effectively train their children? Emotions are a sign that something is wrong. For example, anger comes on the social perception that one is being treated unfairly. Anxiety comes on the perception that there is some danger lurking, and so forth. Understanding emotions as signs from the brain helps us put them into perspective and learn to use them rather than fear them. But like so many other areas of life, how we are trained, by design or default, to deal with emotions in childhood is how we will deal with emotions at any stage of life unless we can learn the critical lessons of effective management. My pain was unbearable and I was unable to share this pain with others, or so I thought. As a child my natural strategy was to run from it, to hide it, to hide from it. It took me a very long time to escape that way of dealing with my demons.

Questions:

As a child how did you deal with your emotions? _____

_____

_____

_____

_____

_____

Did you have anyone to talk to about your feelings? _____

_____

Were emotions discussed in your home growing up? _____

_____

How do you deal with difficult feelings today? _____

_____

_____

_____

_____

_____

Reflections from Jeanne's Journey
Self-blame

There's a subtle difference between blame and responsibility. The concept of blame implies fault. It's a firefighter's responsibility to try to get into that fire and save people. However, if the fire is so fierce that it prevents him from doing that, he is not to blame. The world seems to be divided into people who take no responsibility and others who take too much blame. As a child I was burdened by not knowing the difference between these two concepts. If I couldn't do something it was always my fault. I would beat myself so badly and the pain was so great that I even had suicidal thoughts. My dyslexia was my fault. My anxiety was my fault. You can see how this can very quickly become a self-fulfilling prophecy. Taking the blame can become crippling. It can stop you trying anything for the almost certainty of failure. When you do try, you're always looking over your shoulder waiting for something to go wrong. In short, self-blame is paralyzing.

Questions:

When things go wrong, do you take your share of responsibility?

_____

_____

When things go wrong, do you beat yourself up? _____

_____

_____

Generally, how critical are you of yourself? _____

_____

_____

How critical are you of others? _____

_____

_____

Reflections on Jeanne's Journey
Communication

The ability to talk about one's innermost feelings, isn't about confidence or shyness, it's about trust. One time when I was counseling a couple, the woman complained that her husband never revealed any of his feelings. She was immensely frustrated by this lack of communication and challenged him about it constantly. Indeed, her husband was very quiet and found it almost impossible to talk openly about his emotions. There's a word for that—alexithymic—which has a Greek derivation and literally means "unable to speak about emotions." After a number of sessions, the husband did start expressing some of his feelings for the first time in or out of counseling. As soon as he did, his wife started an intensely critical attack, challenging him on everything he was saying. The man stood up and said, "That's why I never say anything to you," and stomped out of the room. It was a reminder that if you want someone to talk to, you must provide a great communication environment. No one is going to reveal themselves if they think they will be attacked, ridiculed, criticized, abused and disrespected. Neither of my parents gave me that communication environment of trust, which would have allowed me to feel safe in talking to them. As a result, it took me a long time to realize that my communication difficulty wasn't all about me; it was about my lack of trust that I would be taken seriously and really heard.

QUESTIONS:

As a child, did you feel that you could talk to your mother openly about anything? _____

_____

_____

Where there issues that you were actively discouraged from talking about? _____

_____

_____

Did you think you could talk to your father about anything? _____

_____

_____

Were you fearful of talking about your emotions growing up? _____

_____

_____

Do you have anyone that you completely trust so you feel that you could tell them anything? _____

_____

_____

What sort of communication environment do you create for a) partner b) children c) friends d) parents?

Reflections on Jeanne's Journey
A Relationship with God

We all need someone to talk to and we all need someone to trust. When I found that I had few outlets, talking to God was critical. It allowed me to hear myself in prayer, to articulate what I felt and what I wanted. He also gave me hope and the sense that there was a way of viewing the world and my experiences as meaningful. The human mind cannot stand chaos. It requires order and a context for the events that happen to us. Believing that there's a reason and a plan for us is incredibly adaptive. It helps us move forward with confidence, to seek patterns in our lives and to learn from the past. Moreover, a relationship with God helps you rise above your ego and the dictates of the primal brain. In that way, it moves you away from self-pity and resentment and toward compassion and forgiveness.

QUESTIONS:

Do you have a relationship with God? _____

What do you ask God for? _____

_____

_____

_____

_____

_____

_____

What does God ask of you? _____

_____

_____

_____

_____

_____

Do you believe God has a plan for your life? _____

_____

_____

Reflections from Jeanne's Journey
Physical and Emotional Pain

When we are active and feeling fulfilled we typically feel good. That feeling has a biochemical basis. Various neurotransmitters like GABA (Gamma Amino Butyric Acid) which underlies feelings of peace and serenity; dopamine, which is related to pleasure; and oxytocin, associated with feelings of love, are all examples of chemicals that are related to a sense of well-being. Endogenous opiates are also associated with emotional well-being. Conversely, when these chemicals are either low in our system or absent altogether, we feel depressed, despondent and even helpless. Emotional pain, therefore, has physical correlates. And physical pain has emotional correlates.

There is an emotional aspect to hurting physically, which is why anything that can lift our moods, (e.g., relaxation, laughing or being creative) can also help our physical pain. Anything that worsens our moods, (e.g., stress or lack of sleep), will also exaggerate physical pain. This is the reason that opiates are the real "uppers" and why they are so commonly diverted. So, emotional and physical pains are very clearly related which has some implications for pain management.

QUESTIONS:

When you have physical pain, what do you do, if anything, to lift your spirits? _____
_____
_____
_____
_____

When you are under stress, do you also experience physical aches and pains? _____
_____
_____
_____
_____

When you are feeling good emotionally, do you ever experience physical pain? _____
_____
_____
_____
_____

Reflections on Jeanne's Journey
Resilience and Hardship

In the book *Sound Mind Sound Body,* health promotion expert Ken Pelletier describes the health habits of fifty-one famous people. Initially designed to show how successful, busy people take care of themselves, interviews with these celebrities showed that they had one thing in common: almost all of them had a severe setback during their childhood and adolescent years. The conclusion was almost inescapable; setbacks can teach resilience and resilience is necessary for success.

Experiencing shame, humiliation and even disgrace and overcoming obstacles teaches you about more than just faith, hope and perseverance. It teaches you about judgment and the ways people, including ourselves, can view the world in a simplistic, critical and sometimes cruel way. It teaches you not just that you can endure bitterness and resentment but that emotions are temporary and can be overcome. It teaches you that even in the darkest moments, there is always the possibility, even the probability, that the darkness will fade and light will once again shine.

Questions:

What adversities have you had in life? _____

_____

_____

_____

How did you handle them? _____

_____

_____

_____

What did you learn? _____

_____

_____

_____

What would you tell someone going through a difficult time? _____

_____

_____

_____

Reflections from Jeanne's Journey Teaching Through Support

The critical variables that enabled me to get beyond my dyslexia were the support, the nurturing and the belief of my teachers. It should be obvious to anyone that any behavior is learned better through reward than punishment. Punishment only increases the anxiety that someone struggling to learn inevitably feels. Negativity only reinforces the sense of inadequacy. But there's a more important lesson here for learning and education generally. It is obvious but many in education don't realize it or articulate it. I have a friend who is a psychologist and whenever children of all ages came to his practice he asked them one simple question: What is your favorite class in school?

Many children came up with the same response. You have to think outside the box to get the answer but when you do it will be obvious. Hint: the answer is not a subject.

My therapist friend, Jason, has asked this poser of many established educators and those in the education field and few give the right answer. Do you know what most children say is their favorite class?

Children routinely say that their favorite class is…
 the one taught by their favorite teacher.

Jason says: "learning doesn't just occur in the context of a relationship but in the service of it." It wasn't just that my teachers at

Hockaday were supportive and believed in me, they made me want to do my best for them. If you want to get the best out of people, you need a relationship which motivates them to give their best. The old adage comes to mind: "People don't care how much you know until they know how much you care." This is especially true when students are struggling with disabilities or difficulties.

QUESTIONS:

Have you ever had to overcome a disability or a difficulty? _____
_____
_____

What techniques did you use to help you overcome the problem?
_____
_____
_____

What did you learn from the experience? _____
_____
_____
_____

Who helped you and what characteristics did they have that helped you the most? _____

_____

_____

_____

_____

_____

If you had to help someone through a disability or difficulty what would you do? _____

_____

_____

_____

_____

_____

Reflections from Jeanne's Journey
Boundaries

When I stood up to the teacher who tried to humiliate me by showing the class my 'dyslexic' drawing, I was finally feeling worthy enough of standing up for myself.

The development of boundaries is a huge landmark in our lives. Getting those boundaries right can take many years. Some people have no boundaries, which leads to them being hopelessly used and abused. Others have boundaries that are drawn so tight that meaningful relationships are all but impossible. Boundaries can vary depending on the relationship, of course, and a relationship is a dynamic interplay of two people's boundaries.

QUESTIONS:

Do you feel your boundaries are appropriate? _____

_____

Do you feel some people take advantage of you? _____

_____

Do you have a difficult time saying "no"? _____

_____

Reflections on Jeanne's Journey
Guilt

It's a common characteristic that, when you're involved in a traumatic event, you take some responsibility for it. It's like survivor guilt where innocent people regret not taking an action that could conceivably have saved someone else's life. The event is so traumatic that you don't want to believe that it could happen so easily, or that you could be so totally helpless. This mechanism leads to accepting responsibility when none is warranted. In retrospect, I did nothing to encourage my sexual assault nor, once it happened, was there anything I could do about it. Yet, I blamed myself for it.

Sexual consent is still a major issue. Adolescents are not taught about it, the laws about it vary and are often confusing, and the public perception of it is misinformed. If a female goes into her boyfriend's apartment, that is not consent to have sex. If a woman kisses a man, that is not consent. If a woman passes out, that is not consent. The only consent is when a woman actually *states* she agrees to have sex. Nothing else counts as consent, even though many men, and even many women, have a different view. Marital rape and acquaintance rape are still rape and actually represent most of the rape cases in the US, only 26 percent of which are stranger rape. Like many other women, I was left with the feeling that I was somehow to blame. I was too shocked and embarrassed to mention it to anyone; I assumed everyone would see it the same way that I did: I was to blame.

QUESTIONS:

Do you have events in your life that you feel guilt about? _____

_____

Could you really have done something different? _____

_____

Have you been involved in traumatic events? If so, how do you view your role? _____

_____

_____

_____

Have you talked to someone who has shared his or her guilt with you? Did you feel they were being too hard on her/himself? _____

_____

_____

_____

Reflections on Jeanne's Journey
How Can We Be True To Ourselves?

We live in a social world. How others respond to us is so important that we can distort our own thoughts and feelings. How do we know that our thoughts make sense or our feelings are valid? Our self is not independent from the outside world; it resides in it. Successfully integrating our inner experiences with our outer ones is a major component of mental health. How can we safely reveal ourselves? In part, that depends on the belief that you can trust those to whom you are talking. In part, that depends on the ability to trust your own experiences and not deny them or rationalize them away. In part, it depends on having the courage to face the realities of yourself.

Many people don't have a trusted confidante here on earth. People judge, talk, gossip. God doesn't. He doesn't need a privacy policy or require signed consent. He knows your soul. A relationship with God can be the most intimate relationship you will ever have. It is why I had such an exhilarating and personal encounter with Him. Moreover, whomever I would have confidence to confide in on earth wouldn't have been so honest with me. How could I know that another person's comments weren't said to just to make me feel good or to feel bad? How could I know that their reactions to me weren't based on their issues and neuroses?

I could therefore talk to God with complete honesty and know that the answers I received were His desire to lead me to the truth. My truth.

QUESTIONS:

Do you feel comfortable talking honestly about yourself? _____
_____

Who are your confidantes? _____
_____
_____
_____
_____

Are you a good confidante for others? _____
_____

Reflections from Jeanne's Journey
Courage

It takes courage to face yourself. External situations and events will come and go but you are the one constant in your experience. It's so easy and almost natural to attribute our circumstances to the events that happen to us. But as Jim Rohn says: "It's not about making life easier, it's about making me better." And making you better requires being honest with yourself and having the courage to accept who you are. It's fear that prevents us from facing ourselves. But not facing ourselves perpetuates fear. We run, we hide, we rationalize, we avoid. But the moment we stop running, the moment we accept responsibility for ourselves is the moment we get better, the moment we can look ourselves in the eye and know that we are doing our best.

QUESTIONS:

What are your strengths? _____

_____

_____

_____

_____

What are your weaknesses?

Do you believe you really look at yourself in the mirror?

Reflections from Jeanne's Journey
God and Fear

One of the values of faith, and indeed religion in general, is that it can allow you to rise above the limits of the human primitive brain. We can, for example, turn the "other cheek" and we can allow faith to guide us beyond fear. From a brain perspective, fear is heightened brain activity and arousal, technically high beta waves at around 20+ Hz. However, cutting off the fear and reducing the brain activity can take us into a very meditative, peaceful state; one associated with creativity, imagination and visions. This is technically called the alpha/theta boundary because it is at the boundary of these two brain states at around 7 Hz that we fall into this meditative, almost trance-like state. Faith and God, therefore, really allow us to overcome fear and, quite literally, move into a different state of consciousness: one that is beneficial, healing and spiritual.

Fear keeps us from being honest with others and ourselves. It influences our perceptions and our narrative, enabling us to rationalize away difficulties in the pursuit of comfort. How many of us have avoided the real issues because we were afraid of the consequences? By allowing us to defeat fear, God can lead us to honesty and the truth. He literally can shine the light that will illuminate the real issues we are facing.

QUESTIONS:

How do you overcome fear?

What are you fearful of?

Can you think of a time in your life when you avoided facing the real issues?

Reflections on Jeanne's Journey
Drinking and Dependence

The recovery movement is a very significant influence on beliefs about addiction and treatment. Some of these notions can be at odds with the scientific literature. The word "alcoholic" is used in many ways in the popular vernacular. The scientific diagnosis, however, is based on the concept of dependence. There are two types of dependence: physical and psychological. In physical dependence, there are changes at a cellular level so that there is a biological change leading to greater tolerance for alcohol. But with greater tolerance comes the prospect of greater withdrawal when alcohol is not in the system. This increased tolerance and greater withdrawal feeds a cycle leading to more drinking. Now, in scientific terms, dependence lies on a continuum, from mild to severe. One can be mildly, moderately or severely physically dependent. The latter represents more the common stereotype of an alcoholic: one who experiences early morning shakiness as part of withdrawal. The more severe the physical withdrawal, the less control the person will have over his or her drinking, and willpower won't typically be an effective way of avoiding drinking. Psychological dependence also exists on a continuum. Someone who is severely psychologically dependent is likely to reach for the bottle (or other substance) whenever there is emotional discomfort. Clearly, those at the more severe end of the dependence scales are going to have less control over their behavior because of strong biological influences; even if they want to stop it will be harder than those who are less dependent.

Questions:

Have you ever used alcohol or other substance for emotional relief?
_____
_____

How habitual is this behavior? _____
_____
_____

Do you think you are in any way psychologically dependent on alcohol or other substances? _____
_____
_____

Reflections from Jeanne's Journey
Roots and Identity

Most people take their family history for granted, but how critical is it in the formation of identity? It is probably when one doesn't know family history, most common with adoptions, that the question comes into larger focus. Family history does influence a person's sense of identity. This can manifest itself in important information about genetic predispositions, not just for medical conditions but for certain behaviors generally. Cultural and social heritage is critical, too, in helping us understand ourselves. Human beings need narratives that help them put their experiences in context and family history is the narrative that helps us understand ourselves. And, of course, we are important sources of information and example for our own children and future generations.

QUESTIONS:

How much about your ancestors do you know? _____

_____

_____

How much has family history been emphasized in your family?

_____

_____

_____

What activities could you do as family that would shed light on family history? _____

Reflections on Jeanne's Journey
God and Free Will

There's a theory that about 4000 years ago man developed self-consciousness. Julian Jaynes developed that notion more than fifty years ago in his book the *Origin of Consciousness in the Breakdown of the Bicameral Mind*. For the first time in history, the argument goes, man didn't see his thoughts as coming from the gods but were actually his. Thus entered the notion of free will and responsibility. It led to the current notion of God. In this vision, God doesn't act for you. We make our own choices. God, however, helps you deal with the consequences of your own and others' actions. It wasn't God's role to stop me from making stupid decisions. He helped me to change and heal from those decisions and my subsequent actions.

God gave me the courage through faith to face my issues. I did pray for God to "make everything right" but He taught me that I am the only one who can do that. Faith requires action. Or more accurately, I am the only one who can direct my decisions and my behavior. He was there to provide counsel, guidance and sometimes open doors for intervention that I could choose to walk through. Just handing the responsibility over to Him wasn't going to work. My belief in God helped me do what I needed to do for transformation and enlightenment. My faith led to forgiveness and to healing.

Questions:

When you pray, what do you ask God for? _____

_____

_____

_____

Do you pray for solutions or strength, enlightenment and courage?

_____

Have you ever had an awakening in which you suddenly saw life from a different perspective? _____

_____

How did that come about? What did you do about it? _____

_____

_____

_____

_____

Have you ever blamed someone or something else for your own thoughts or choices? _____

_____

Who or what did you blame? _____

_____

_____

_____

How does passing the blame resolve anything? _____

_____

_____

_____

Reflections from Jeanne's Journey
Rock Bottom

In the addictions and the recovery movement, there's the notion of 'Rock Bottom': the moment when life gets so painful that continuing with the status quo is no longer tolerable. The problem with this feeling is that it can be temporary. Today's shame and guilt can be rationalized away tomorrow as the product of bad luck or unfortunate circumstances and the pain is never converted into energy for healing. This is especially true in the grip of addiction and/or the throes of withdrawal. People can be highly motivated to change one day and be disinclined to change the next.

Two psychologists, James Prochaska and Carlo DiClemente worked in the addiction field thirty years ago. In recognition of the fact that addicts in or out of treatment are at different stages of motivation, they set about creating a guide to motivational stages. Their five-stage model is helpful for thinking about motivation for any change, not just in the addictions. Their model consists of the five phases:

> *Precontemplation:* where there is no recognition of the need to change, sometimes called 'denial.'
>
> *Contemplation:* where there is a recognition of the need to change but no action or commitment.
>
> *Preparedness:* where the person is making active plans to change.

Action: where new behavior is instituted.

Maintenance: where effective action is maintained.

These stages provide a very useful framework for understanding your, or anyone else's, motivation. Research, as well as common sense, suggests that people don't move smoothly through these stages. People can be stuck in one stage or another for years (e.g. precontemplation) and then suddenly commit to and quickly move through the stages (contemplation and preparedness) to action.

Also, one can also move in the reverse direction. You can be in the action phase, get discouraged and slide all the way back to precontemplation.

The model was designed to determine what are the most effective messages to help someone along from the stage they are currently in. What Prochaska and DiClemente observed was that health professionals typically assumed that addicts they were helping were all in the action phase, which clearly wasn't accurate. What someone needs in the contemplation phase, for example, is different than what he or she needs in the action phase. In the contemplation phase, one needs exposure to people who have had similar experiences and succeeded, a vision of what actions will look like and reminders of the penalties of staying in the same destructive routines. In the action phase, one needs support, reinforcement, accountability and things that will facilitate new behavior.

QUESTIONS:

Do you need to make a change in your life? _____

_____

If so, where in the five-stage model of motivation are you currently?

_____

_____

_____

If you're not in the action phase, what can you do to get there?

_____

_____

_____

Reflections on Jeanne's Journey Narcissism and Self-Preservation

The word "selfish" has a very negative connotation because the concept is itself confusing. The word implies "focusing on the self" which generally is assumed to be a bad characteristic. However, there are clearly times when focusing on oneself is a very important and healthy thing to do. The core concept and the real issue is whether this selfishness is an occasional behavior necessary for self-preservation or a constant absorption with self. Obviously, there is a vast difference. When people talk about selfish in a negative way, they are more accurately talking about narcissism, which implies self-absorption. Moreover, such self-absorption is a constant characteristic.

There are times when it is appropriate to be selfish, but narcissism is never appropriate. Nonetheless, this doesn't stop people from firing the accusatory "you're being selfish." (People often say this when you're not doing the things they want you to do). For the sensitive person, selfishness is a bad thing. This concept makes her feel guilty if she takes time for herself, or thinks about herself or her feelings. It leads her to minimize or even dishonor her feelings and her thoughts. It is really critical to distinguish between the healthy need for selfishness and the destructiveness of narcissism.

It is hard for people to make the switch out of selflessness. Guilt and even anxiety automatically emerge when doing things for oneself. But someone who has spent many years in selflessness is not going to become narcissistic. Imagine a scale that runs from selflessness at one end to narcissism at the other. A selfless person can change and, hopefully, he or she will move toward the middle of that scale. But there's virtually no chance of them going from one end to the other, from selflessness to narcissism. In fact, the formerly selfless person has to work very hard indeed to recognize the importance and necessity of self-care.

QUESTIONS:

Do you take care of your personal needs? How? _____

_____

_____

_____

_____

If not, what do you neglect? _____

_____

_____

_____

Do you ever feel guilty for taking some time for yourself? _____

_____

Reflections from Jeanne's Journey
Compassion and Codependency

Where does compassion end and codependency begin? There are some important distinctions here. One is between feeling and behavior. You might empathize with someone but that doesn't mean you have to DO anything about their plight. It's their plight not yours. Compassion is the ability to feel what others are feeling. It does not imply doing anything. Compassion is a natural sense of identification with others. We are hardwired through our mirror neuron system to be able to identify with others. Some of us have ultradeveloped compassion where we can identify with everyone to a very intense degree.

Codependency is the illusion that we're helping someone when we're basically interfering in his or her life and allowing a negative behavior to continue. Codependency can be born out of a need to control or can come out of a need for love and attention. Sometimes, codependency comes from a fear of conflict and the need for peace.

A key word here is boundaries. Through your compassion, you can feel someone's pain and see that they need help. Someone with good boundaries can explain to the person what they see, why help is needed and where to get it. But good boundaries mean that person is not going to provide the help. Obviously, I am not talking about an immediate crisis involving a physical emergency where someone's life is at risk. Then, hopefully you would do all that you reasonably could to help, but not at the expense of your own life. For example, if you saw someone drowning in quicksand, throwing him a rope is a compassionate act, jumping into the quicksand with him is a codependent act and a stupid one.

At the heart of ending codependency is knowing that while you may identify others' problems, you can't solve them; they have to. That's a difficult realization but an essential one.

QUESTIONS:

Do you have good boundaries? _____

_____

Do you often feel that you are giving yourself and your time away?

_____

Do you feel guilty when you say "no"? _____

_____

Reflections on Jeanne's Journey
Death of a Parent

Regardless of the relationship you have had with a parent, his or her passing is a critical life milestone. For better or for worse, parents are in your life, even when they are not physically present. Parents are literally and metaphorically embedded in your DNA, influencing your actions, choices and behaviors. They can be directly responsible, through genetics, example or encouragement, for your triumphs and your failures, your health and your sicknesses, your strengths and your weaknesses.

The vast percentage of parents tried their best for their children. Except for the really sick ones, children were the recipients of their parents' most loving moments and their highest aspirations. Parents have their weaknesses and their neuroses and every one will have made mistakes. But when a parent dies, there's part of the child that goes with them.

Regardless of your relationship with your parents, your last days and moments with them are a special time unlike any other. When a parent is on the edge of crossing over, there is no tomorrow. There may not be an afternoon or an evening. There may not be the opportunity to say much or anything at all. And sometimes, you don't have to say anything. It's about being there.

QUESTIONS:

If you have experienced the loss of a parent, what did you do? Would you do anything differently? _____

_____

_____

_____

_____

If you have children, how do you want to be remembered? _____

_____

_____

_____

_____

If you have important things to tell your children, what are you waiting for? _____

_____

_____

_____

_____

Reflections from Jeanne's Journey
Marriage, the Second Time

No matter what people may tell you, it's very hard not to be influenced by your first marriage; and you should be. Marriage and cohabitation require a very specific set of skills and attitudes to be successful. Hopefully, by the time you get to a second marriage, you have matured and know yourself better. That allows you to be clearer about what you want in a partner and a soul mate. The fact is that people change, often dramatically, during their twenties. Priorities, vision, goals and self-understanding all change and develop over time. In my case, I came to these understandings as my marriage was failing, and, even after I had divorced David. However, you don't have to wait until your marriage is failing to address these critical questions.

A marriage is a dynamic relationship that goes through transitions. Your goals at fifty are going to be different than they are at thirty. It is important, therefore, to constantly review your vision, goals and purpose throughout the different stages of life with or without a spouse. If you don't know where you're going or what you want, how can you decide on the appropriate partner or guide your partner if you have one?

Questions:

What are your needs? _____

_____

_____

_____

_____

_____

What are your goals? _____

_____

_____

_____

_____

_____

What do the above imply about the type of partner best suited to you?

_____

_____

_____

_____

_____

Reflections from Jeanne's Journey
The "Truth"

Life is not a math quiz and often the answers are as obscure as the questions. Truth comes in all shapes and sizes, forms and contexts and it comes at different times. When we are in the midst of conflict, our brain's main goal is survival, not accuracy. We are concerned with self-protection, not objectivity. As a result, our perspective is biased and our judgments can be flawed. The problem is that those instant judgments form our perceptions and those perceptions become our memories and are encoded as the truth. It takes courage to face those perceptions with the knowledge that they could be flawed. It is almost impossible to explore them on your own; self-analysis can only go so far until it collides with itself. There's the value of the other person, the one who is not invested in survival, the one who can be more analytical because it is not his own self, it's yours.

It's hard to reshape our narratives. Each story and every perception are bricks on which others are built. There's the serious risk that if too many bricks are removed, the whole scaffolding of your truth collapses. That is too scary; it is better to be wrong than to be lost. But when you admit to other possibilities, when you can see beyond your hurt and self-protection, and admit that your perception of others didn't allow for weaknesses, imperfections, hurts, traumas and pain, then you can see a different kind of truth. And that is a truth that will set you free.

QUESTIONS:

When you make negative judgments about people are you ever aware that you might be wrong? _____

_____

Have you ever changed a negative valuation of someone? If so, why?

_____

_____

_____

_____

_____

Do you think that anyone has ever misjudged you? How? _____

_____

_____

_____

_____

_____

Reflections from Jeanne's Journey
Regret

It is very difficult, if not impossible, for humans to be objective. It is the nature of things for humans to be wrong, misguided and simplistic. The answer does not lie in perfection but in recognition of the fact that we can't be objective. We make mistakes and misjudge people; at best, our perceptions are one-sided. Being open to the possibilities of our interpretations and judgments, and being ready and willing to rectify, apologize and forgive is the way to accommodate for the way our brains work.

Perhaps that is the nature of wisdom: the recognition of the process and the understanding that just because a thought or a perception forms in our mind, it is not automatically right, true or acceptable. So don't regret, but understand the process and be ready to rectify your perceptions when necessary. In fact, regret is recognition of the process.

QUESTIONS:

Do you take the time and effort to consider whether your judgments and perceptions are accurate? _____

_____

_____

If you realize they are inaccurate do you try to rectify them publicly, (e.g., apologize)? _____

_____

_____

How do you respond when people reach out to you and admit they may have misjudged you? _____

_____

_____

_____

_____

_____

_____

Reflections from Jeanne's Journey
Anger Management

You will recall the agony and pain I endured from what seemed like a botched surgery after my mother died. I consulted an attorney who seemed to believe I had a strong case. However, I chose not to pursue it. Was that a poor decision? Was it a cop-out or was it wisdom personified? I think of it as the latter.

It would have been easy to focus my anger and frustration on the doctors involved in that particular surgery and rehabilitation. And it is likely it would not have cost me any money as the attorney was willing to take the case on a contingency basis. But it was the other costs that were important to me. My case would likely have dragged on for years. During that time, I would be continually faced with my anger, frustration and pain. Even if my pain disappeared, which it eventually did, I would still be reliving it every time I spoke to my attorney, looked at the inevitable mountain of documents or went to court. And I believe that subconsciously my body would have amplified the pain because I would be living out the role of victim. Compensation neurosis is the term for people who consciously exaggerate their injuries when they are involved in legal disputes of this nature. But the body and mind are inextricably linked, so subconscious mechanisms are at work, too, and are likely to conspire to create the role: in this case, a victim with intractable pain.

So I am very relieved that I made the decision not to walk down the path of litigation. I had to exercise considerable control over my emotions and my desire for justice. It was a hard-fought battle but one where wisdom prevailed.

There was one other factor that helped me in my decision. It is not my position to judge others. That is for God, not me. I was once again rescued by my relationship with God. He would take care of it, allowing me to focus on recovery and the next part of my journey.

QUESTIONS:

When you get mad with people, do you always feel that you have to get even with them? _____

_____

_____

When you are emotional or upset about something, do you ever stop to weigh the personal costs to you of pursuing a course of action?

_____

_____

Has an emotional reaction ever backfired on you? _____

_____

_____

Reflections on Jeanne's Journey
Dreams and Symbols

The notion that people think logically has been debunked by research. Rather, we are much more "intuitive" than perhaps we like to admit. In his book *Thinking Fast and Slow,* Nobel Prize-winner Daniel Kahneman entertainingly describes the cognitive research and shows how two different processes, that he calls System 1 and System 2, guide our thinking and problem-solving. System 1 thinking is by far the most predominant. It involves a combination of emotion, memory and some fast rational analysis of a few critical variables to generate a thought that is really more intuition than logic. System 1 is fast, simple and relatively easy. It generates thoughts, decisions and stories that are consistent with all our other stories, thoughts and perceptions, and that "feel right."

System 2 thinking, on the other hand, is hard work. It entails the application of logic and statistical rules. You are using System 2 thinking when you are doing a math calculation (not on a machine) or doing a statistical analysis. System 2 is like switching into thinking in a different language. System 2 is also stressful. When you are using your brain in this way, it absorbs all of your focus and the fight-flight system is activated. As a result, most of us avoid using System 2 if at all possible. Moreover, most people are not trained in effective logical analysis unless they pursue a science career or become an engineer.

System 1 thinking, then, depends on access to our past memories and experiences, many of which are subconscious. The fact is that, when we are exposed to a situation, all of our relevant memories and associated emotions are activated to create our narratives, perceptions and thoughts. This happens very quickly and almost always without conscious awareness.

This is one reason why it is important to access those memories and ideas that lay beyond the conscious. They are influencing how we react to the world and define ourselves. They are at the core of our thinking and every decision we make. How do we access the unconscious?

One natural way is through dreams. Our dreams represent aspects of our unconscious; they are indeed a window on the ideas and feelings that drive us. Dreams also come to us in a way that allows us to revisit our habitual conscious processes and thought patterns. In a way, dreams are just another example of System 1 thinking, but thinking freed from the limitations of consciousness and thinking habit. Dreams and symbols help to free us from self-imposed limitations. Dreams provide an intimate connection between your interior and exterior life. Dreams are gifts of wisdom that come to us in the night.

Because they allow us to escape conscious constraints and explore new stories about ourselves, dreams help us to build new boundaries or to repair broken ones. Dreams help us to turn around and to see where we have been. Dreams tend to shatter false illusions. Dreams heal broken, torn and wounded places in our lives.

Dreams reflect our experiences and, as a result, they are as unique as our fingerprints. There are various qualities of dreams that are important.

Dreams emphasize their importance through symbols. Although words can be heard in a dream, the visual imagery is more important. The emphasis on symbols rather than spoken language is just an extension of the fact that, even when consciously processing the spoken word, we focus more on the visual and other cues of the speaker. A picture is indeed worth a thousand words because our brain is more attuned to image than to word. We use System 1 gut feel to interpret what people are saying to us, not System 2 logical analysis of their speech.

Because we are fundamentally intuitive, the emotional tone of the dream is critical. For example, you might recall that, in chapter fifteen, I write about a dream I had in which I was confronted by a bear. But instead of the emotion of the dream being one of fear, it was one of love. If I had exactly the same dream but the emotion had been fear, the meaning of the dream would have been completely different. Whenever you do have a scary dream, you need to pay attention! Your subconscious is telling you something that either you hadn't consciously registered, or had, but not to the right degree.

Emotions, wherever they occur, are warnings. Fear in a dream is an invitation to consider the situation and determine how great the threat is. Fear in a dream doesn't necessarily mean you should be terrified, but rather your subconscious is giving you a warning signal.

We interpret our dreams with System 1 intuitive thinking. In that respect, it is valuable to muse about all aspects of the dream and pay close attention to what comes into your mind. A dream can't be subject to System 2 thinking. It is not a math question. It reveals its meaning through intuition, not logic. We look through and down into the dream to see new possibilities.

So, follow your dream images wherever they may lead.

As you have read above, our conscious System 1 thinking is programmed to lead us to oversimplistic, comfortable perceptions. Dreams can provide a subtlety that our everyday conscious-thinking often eschews. Dreams show our shadows even if they are barely recognizable.

As well as musing about dreams, try to reenter them. If you close your eyes and try to reimagine the dream, what thoughts and feelings arise? Have a conversation with the characters in your dream.

The symbols and images in a dream have a relationship with one another. The nature of those relationships in any particular dream is important.

QUESTIONS:

Do you remember your dreams? _____

_____

Do you ever stop to consider your dreams? _____

_____

Has anything important ever been revealed to you in a dream?

Reflections on Jeanne's Journey
Forgiveness

Forgiveness is an important part of self-awareness and of leading a fulfilled life. Think about what happens when you perceive that someone has wronged you in some way. Typically, you will get angry and quite possibly have a variety of revenge fantasies, designed to help you feel in control of the situation as well as vent your frustration.

So, you are now in an emotional state, which as we have seen, will influence your perceptions and narrative. System 1 thinking will mean that you are likely to create a narrative driven by your emotion rather than your judgment. Not only is this likely to be distorted, it is going to be stressful, time-consuming, distracting and energy consuming.

It is often pointed out that when you get to this stage, not only is this an unproductive state but that you are also still allowing the offending person to control you, even if they have no idea that they are. This is a perfect scenario for the offender, having an impact on you without expending one calorie's worth of effort.

So, sure, letting go of the anger and allowing yourself to forgive is an act that is very self-protective. But forgiveness is so much more than that.

In many ways, forgiveness is the opposite of judgment. Rather than being critical and allowing System 1 thinking to generate oversimplistic stories that focus on the negative, forgiveness does the reverse. It allows you to not just let go of the emotion but also the thought process that underpins it.

The most difficult act of forgiveness for me was forgiving myself. It felt like I was letting myself off too easily and avoiding the issue. In time, I saw that if I could forgive others then I could forgive myself. When I thought and prayed about it, I knew that God had forgiven me. If He could, so could I. This self-forgiveness allowed me to move on. Now I have to say that if I forgave myself for an action that was hurtful to either myself and/or others, and kept doing that action, then forgiveness would be neither real nor helpful. You can't forgive hurtful actions that continue. That's not forgiveness, that's codependency and self-harm.

Letting go is one of the hardest activities for human beings to do, but also the most liberating. Forgiveness is the ultimate exercise in letting go and, as a result, is great practice in the difficult and valuable skill of exercising conscious restraint on your thoughts and emotions.

QUESTIONS:

Have you ever forgiven anyone? _____

_____

_____

Has anyone forgiven you? How did that feel?

Have there been instances where your forgiveness could have made a difference in your life or the lives of others?

Reflections on Jeanne's Journey
Laughter

I have found laughter to be healing in many different ways. For one thing, when you are laughing, you can't feel any negative emotions. The physical act of laughing, and even smiling, seems to temporarily prohibit any feelings of tension or stress. Laughter may be even more healing than we imagine and go beyond the temporary inhibition of anxiety.

In his book *Anatomy of an Illness,* Norman Cousins describes how he used laughter to help him heal from the serious condition of ankylosing spondylitis, an illness that affects the connective tissue in the spinal cord. On the assumption that if negative emotions produce negative changes in the body, positive emotions would produce positive chemical changes, Cousins devised his treatment around creating such positive emotions. He found that laughter, induced in his case by watching, among other things Marx Brothers movies and the TV show "Candid Camera," indeed had a positive effect. Ten minutes of belly laughter had an anesthetic effect and promoted uninterrupted sleep. We now know that laughter boosts the immune system, reduces stress and boosts endorphins giving us a sense of well-being.

There is a notion that children laugh a lot more than adults, although some research questions this. Research has shown that laughter is much more likely to occur in social situations and indeed, recognizing the value of a good laugh, there are therapeutic clubs set up to encourage the social expression of humor.

In any event, laughter is clearly very therapeutic and the risk is that we don't do it enough. Apart from trying to lighten up generally and see the humor in things, you can make efforts to increase your exposure to humorous movies, books and other sources. Increasing social interaction with fun-loving friends would also help.

QUESTIONS:

*How often do you laugh a day on average?*_____

_____

*When was the last time you had a real belly laugh?*_____

_____

List five people you know who really make you laugh:

_____

_____

_____

_____

Reflections on Jeanne's Journey
Reframing Disasters

"Life can only be understood backwards but you've got to live it forwards," said the Danish philosopher Soren Kierkegaard. How true that is. Often, the many struggles I had in my life turned out not to be the road to hell that they seemed at the time but rather the path to enlightenment.

I have come to truly embrace the notion that it's not what happens to you but how you handle those events that determine your destiny. At many turns in my life, when I felt I couldn't take any more, I was inspired to find truth and seek a better path. Perhaps our most difficult moments inspire us to find meaning that we don't search for when life is treating us well.

The pattern of finding meaning in the most difficult times has been repeated so often in my life that when difficulties arise now I instinctively see them as opportunities for growth and enlightenment. I see them as milestones on my spiritual journey.

The issue here is about seeking meaning, positive meaning, from everything that happens in your life. It's not just "everything happens for a reason;" it is just that "everything happens for a good reason." But in order to embrace that idea, especially when life is tough, you have to have faith. If tough times inspire you to have faith, then they are worth their weight in gold. By inspiring faith in both a Higher Power and yourself, life difficulties are a blessing, even though they may not seem it at the time.

QUESTIONS:

How do you deal with crises in your life? _____

_____

_____

_____

_____

_____

_____

When crises happen do you stress out or are you able to deal with them effectively? _____

_____

Have you ever had something happen, which, at the time, you thought was a disaster but later turned out to be a blessing? _____

_____

Reflections on Jeanne's Journey
Gratitude

Looking at the blessings in my life, rather than the obstacles, made a huge difference for me. Gratitude does indeed change your mind-set. Human beings are fickle and it's very easy for us to take our circumstances for granted. Even when confronted with evidence, which should make us take a conscious look at our blessings, we often don't. For example, you might see a news feature about families in refugee camps, displaced by war and struggling to get enough food to eat. But very few people would take that image and idea to heart. We're likely to go to the refrigerator or out to dinner without much of a thought, let alone an emotional connection, to the idea that we are fortunate to have a choice of foods whenever we want.

Gratitude changes that perception and makes us consciously pay attention to our blessings because, from the example above, it can be seen that we're not going to gratuitously connect with the idea of deprivation unless we either experience it ourselves or force ourselves to focus on it.

I make it a practice each day to be thankful for all the wonderful gifts I have. It's amazing what happens when you do that. It's not just that you are more appreciative of your obvious blessings; you start to see blessings where you hadn't before. With a gratitude mind-set, you realize the value in many things as you change the mental scale by which events are evaluated. This stems from the work on System 1 thinking and, especially, the notion of "anchoring." If you focus on negative events, everything becomes judged in terms of negativity. If you focus on positive events, life becomes evaluated in terms of its benefits.

QUESTIONS:

What do you have gratitude for? _____

_____

_____

_____

_____

Do you ever stop to count your blessings? _____

_____

How could you express gratitude? _____

_____

_____

_____

_____

Reflections on Jeanne's Journey Exploring Nature

I have found being in nature very comforting and therapeutic. Whether by mountains or in the woods, by the ocean or on a lake, the beauty of nature speaks to my soul. The key here is to focus on the nature when you're in it. There's no point going for a walk in the woods if you're going to be on your cellphone. To really appreciate it, you need to consciously pay attention to it. Surround yourself in it.

It's so easy to get wrapped up in our lives and not take time to appreciate the beauty around us. Appreciating the beauty of the natural world will help to inspire gratitude (see above) and take us out of mind-sets that are restricted by the mundane and the everyday.

We take nature so much for granted and human beings often view it from a very selfish angle. Have you ever seen a magnificent tree being cut down? Have you seen the wonders of its growth reduced to logs on the ground? Have you ever really paid attention to a flock of birds flying in formation across the evening sky? Have you ever looked at the night sky through a telescope? When you do these activities, you will start to see your home, the planet you live on, in a different light. Really being in nature can be a mind-set changer as it helps us get away from our selfish perspectives and see the bigger picture. And seeing the bigger picture is about recognizing that there are forces greater than ourselves in the universe. For me, being in nature is a spiritual walk.

QUESTIONS:

When was the last time you took the time to experience nature?

_____

_____

What activities could you do to connect with the natural world?

_____

_____

_____

_____

_____

What was your best experience in nature? _____

_____

_____

_____

_____

Reflections on Jeanne's Journey
Therapy

By definition, self-analysis is only possible to a degree. There are times when we need the input of others to help clarify our feelings, thoughts and behavior. Friends and relatives can be helpful but, generally, they are not independent or neutral. A competent therapist can help you identify your issues as well as give you support and strategies for change.

There are various forms of therapy but all aim to give you insight that can then be used as the basis of change. Some therapy focuses on your relationships, some on your thoughts, others on emotions and behaviors and some on all of these. Individual therapy is also founded on developing a good relationship with a therapist that is built on trust and mutual respect. In reality, it is hard to find people whom you could entrust yourself to. If you have one really good friend, you're doing well; and even that friendship isn't the same as a therapeutic relationship.

When looking for therapists, don't be shy about being discerning. Ask mental health professionals about their credentials, experiences and the types of cases they prefer to work with. If you don't feel comfortable with one, keep looking for others who might be a better match for you.

Questions:

Have there been times in your life when you wished you had a professional confidante? _____

_____

Do you have the support in your life that you need? _____

_____

Do you know your strengths and weaknesses and what to do about them? _____

_____

_____

Reflections on Jeanne's Journey
Creativity

I have found that the creative process is very healing and been a critical part of my journey. For one thing, the creative brain state is quite different from the rational and sensory processing that goes on much of the time. The creative state requires a much lower level of arousal and the ability to stop processing. This brain state is much closer to meditation than normal consciousness. Not only is this very relaxing, it accesses a part of ourselves that can easily get lost in the mayhem of everyday life.

In addition, self-expression is very important. Creative outlets allow us to express our thoughts and feelings differently and not necessarily through the rational, logical filter. This allows access to thoughts and feelings that might otherwise be inaccessible. This creative expression of ourselves allows us to not only find greater self-expression but possibly release feelings that otherwise are left unexplored and unexpressed.

People vary in their creative abilities but all of us can manifest creative expression. The purpose of being creative isn't necessarily to produce a great work of art but to access and exercise a very important part of ourselves.

QUESTIONS:

How often do you do a creative activity? _____

Name at least three creative activities that you have interest in doing:

As an adult have you ever taken a class in creative pursuit, (e.g., a musical instrument, photography, arts and crafts, creative writing, etc.)? _____

Reflections on Jeanne's Journey
Telling Your Story

The story we have about ourselves impacts our perceptions, thoughts, feelings and behavior. Often we don't examine that narrative, or update it based on new experiences and insights. Writing is thinking, and writing about yourself is a valuable experience which will almost certainly give you new insights and perceptions about your life, identity and purpose.

I have talked about the value of keeping a journal, but this writing is very specifically geared to reconstructing your life story, rather than writing about your current experiences. I have found that writing about my life enabled me to review old thoughts and habitual perceptions which had outlived their usefulness and no longer reflected my reality. Indeed, they were instrumental in me maintaining a negative and distorted view of myself.

The purpose of writing your story is for the discovery and insight that will follow when you look at your life through a different lens. You may or may not want to put your thoughts into a book; getting published is not the purpose of the exercise.

If writing is too daunting for you, you could dictate your thoughts into a recording device, and if you so wanted, could have transcripts made of your voice recordings.

Here are some tips for writing your story:

1. Begin by writing a timeline of your life: birth to present day.
2. Identify the main periods of your life by age, topic or time.
3. Detail the main events of the period and the elements that make up the plot of your personal story.
4. Describe the situation and your role. What went particularly well and what special challenges did you overcome? What special talents did you use?
5. Include the physical, psychological and spiritual highs and lows of each period.
6. Describe the people in your life and your relationship to them.
7. What values were met and which were challenged or threatened?
8. Examine the major discoveries and the insights of each period or each event that has occurred as you have moved along on your journey.
9. Indicate those points where you feel that your story has been significantly bisected by the Divine story.

I hope the reflections that come from your journey are as meaningful to you as mine have been for me.

Good luck and God Bless!

About the Author

Jeanne Miller is an accomplished psychotherapist, spiritual director, author and award-winning photographer. Holding a master's degree and professional license in social work, she has been a practicing therapist in a variety of settings including inpatient and outpatient psychiatric care facilities, an adoption agency, a physical rehabilitation center and in private practice. She has a special interest and training in dream studies.

Jeanne is the author of two previous books: *Dream Symbols in Waking Life* and *Lives Interrupted: The Unwanted Pregnancy Dilemma.* An avid photographer, Jeanne has had some of her work on display in Three Columns Gallery, Harvard University and galleries in Texas, California and Vermont.

CPSIA information can be obtained
at www.ICGtesting.com
Printed in the USA
LVOW02s1452030516
486487LV00008B/36/P